D1758047

# VISUAL FAMILIES

*GRAPHIC STORYTELLING IN DESIGN AND ILLUSTRATION*

gestalten

# INTRODUCTION

*BY NOELIA HOBEIKA*

At first glance, **Visual Families** is a lighthearted collection of visual groupings, yet there is more than meets the eye. The common thread among these works is indeed the intention to tie a variety of related items together in an aesthetically pleasing way, but while some are straightforwardly informative or decorative pieces, others are subtly provocative, sometimes even masquerading as cheerful illustrations. Whether designed to provide information, make a point, or tell a story, or designed just for the love of drawing, all of the works featured in this book invite the viewer to take a closer look—to appreciate elaborate graphics and humorous captioning, or to detect a hidden meaning.

Form and content play equally important parts in the creation of such works. The fact that the format of these visual families is somewhat restricted puts these pieces on equal footing and provides a productive limitation on their composition. With the same starting point in terms of format, designers and illustrators are then free to play with composition, some preferring to employ a classic grid format and others choosing to experiment with less clearly organized presentations. Somewhere in between the two, you can find pieces that replicate natural history museum display cases, a popular choice for prints depicting a group of insects or plants, such as Kyler Martz's "Butterflies" (p. 36). Even in a seemingly simple arrangement such as an A-Z format, there is always room for innovation, as demonstrated by Hugo Yoshikawa's "European Cities ABC" (p. 96), in which each city's notable monuments and symbols have been intricately shaped into the corresponding letter of the alphabet.

These various kinds of compositions are the basis of a visual language that has become a prevalent storytelling technique. Indeed, we encounter visual family graphics every day in magazines, on the internet, or on billboards; the creatives behind them understand that they are an effective method for viewers to process information. The way these images are structured allows us to better comprehend certain ideas and see things through a new lens—a perfect platform to communicate a message. It is therefore no surprise that more and more of these groupings are being commissioned to illustrate articles, such as Francesco Muzzi's "Who Is Working At Home?" (p. 100), which was published in **Bulletin** magazine alongside an article about the division of domestic work among married couples in Switzerland.

As an eye-catching, succinct platform to pass on information, the visual family is also the perfect medium to communicate thought-provoking commentary. It has great potential to spark curiosity in viewers, encouraging them to look more closely and perhaps confront controversial topics. London-based artist Adam Simpson's "Personalised Medicine" (p. 115) is a great example: using a deceivingly cheerful aesthetic with vivid colors, Simpson's piece matches a group of people with their corresponding pills—a compelling argument about today's compulsive behavior towards medication.

Provocation comes in many forms, including humor, which is extremely effective in opening the way for discussion on polemical subjects. Christoph Niemann employed this technique when creating "The Real Empires of Evil" (p. 124), an illustration commissioned by alternative political magazine **Nozone** showing a grid of re-designed national flags to match their newly attributed names, such as "Burger Kingdom" for the U.K. and "The United States of Amnesia" for the U.S.A.

As a newly widespread mode of storytelling, visual groupings are a significant part of everyone's visual vocabulary today. **Visual Families** invites you to become even more well-versed in this form of gripping communication: some arouse further discussion on political subjects, others scientifically catalog nature, and many obsessively assemble mundane items, but all encourage viewers to examine them more closely, sometimes leading to unexpected conclusions when scratching their surface.

HAVE YOU EVER BEEN TO
MILANO
DUBLINO
LAS VEGAS
VENEZIA
Marsiglia
SALT LAKE CITY
Amsterdam
REYKJAVIK
NIZZA
Bordeaux
SINGAPORE
CHICAGO
Siviglia
LOS ANGELES
MIAMI
HONOLULU
AUSTIN
bali
WASHINGTON
LA PAZ
OSAKA
MONTE CARLO
SAN FRANCISCO
BELGRADO
ASPEN
DES MOINES
NAIROBI
COLOMBO
VANCOUVER
CITTÀ DEL MESSICO
ZURIGO
HOUSTON
ROMA
BERLINO
PECHINO
BARCELONA
Genova
PRAGA
mumbai
VARSAVIA
MOSCA
istanbul
NEW YORK
HONG KONG
TOKYO
LIMA
TAIPEI
GOTHAM CITY
RIO DE JANEIRO
VIENNA
Hokkaidō
TORONTO
OSLO
nuovadelhi
LONDRA
Lisbona
ASTANA
GLASGOW
Oxford
MELBOURNE
L'AVANA
HELSINKI
KINGSTON
Casablanca
SIDNEY
CITTÀ DEL CAPO
MADRID
SANTORINI
Il Cairo
BLACKPOOL
KUALA LUMPUR
NIAGARA FALLS
CALCUTTA
MONTREAL
NEW ORLEANS
DUBAI
SAN PIETROBURGO
Jerez
ATENE
COPENAGHEN
PARIGI
La Mecca
Marrakech
BERGEN

• CHECK THE SPACES NEAR THE CITIES YOU HAVE BEEN. DONE? GOOD. NOW HURRY UP AND FINISH THE WORLD! START TODAY! •

**RESERVOIR DOGS**

**THE BIG LEBOWSKI**

**THE GREAT GATSBY**

**ROMEO & JULIET**

**FEDERICA BONFANTI**
*HAVE YOU EVER BEEN TO, 2012*

Federica Bonfanti has taken care of your bucket list: "Have You Ever Been To" is a poster depicting 84 places that the illustrator thinks you should see before you die.

**KYLE TEZAK**
*FOUR ICON CHALLENGE, 2011*

Kyle Tezak simplifies narratives into four icons that express basic plots. What started as a design challenge became a way for the designer to identify and catalog themes that drive some of his favorite stories.

ATHENS
BUDAPEST
CAPE TOWN
DUBAI
EDINBURGH
FRANKFURT
GENEVA
HONG KONG
ISTANBUL
JERUSALEM
KYOTO
LOS ANGELES
MOSCOW
NEW YORK
OAXACA
PARIS
QUITO
ROME
SIEM REAP
TORONTO
UTRECHT
VIENNA
WELLINGTON
XIENG KHOUANG
YANGON
ZAGREB

**BURLESQUE
OF NORTH AMERICA**
*WORLD TRAVEL ALPHABET PRINT 2013*

To arouse curiosity about the world and its most iconic monuments, Mike Davis designed this screen print as a gift for his nephew Lazlo. Davis chose 26 cities from around the world, one for each letter of the alphabet, and illustrated their major landmarks with bright colors using stylized lines that appeal to both children and adults.

# FIFTEEN POPULAR HEADWEAR STYLES FOR GENTLEMEN

BALMORAL BONNET

TOP HAT

HOMBERG

KEPI

PANAMA

SOU'WESTER

BOATER

FEZ

DEERSTALKER

BOWLER

PITH HELMET

TYROLEAN HAT

CASQUETTE

PORK PIE

BEANIE HAT

**JAMES BROWN LTD.**
*HATS, 2010*

This five-color screen print presents 15 different headwear styles for men, from the timeless panama to the oh-so-fancy top hat.

**JAMES PROVOST**
*MID-CENTURY MODERN HOMES & MID-CENTURY MODERN FURNITURE, 2012/2009*

To the left is a collection of iconic mid-century modern homes by James Provost that was commissioned by **Arts & Architecture** magazine. Designers represented include Frank Lloyd Wright, Ludwig Mies van der Rohe, and Le Corbusier. To the right, Provost created a poster of iconic mid-century modern furniture that one can imagine has decorated the homes to the left, such as Jacobsen's famous "Egg Chair" and Charles & Ray Eames's "Eames Lounge" chair.

**BURLESQUE
OF NORTH AMERICA**
*TOOLS OF THE TRADE, FALL 2012*

**JORDON CHEUNG**
*17 DAYS OF SUMMER, 2012*

Once upon a time, we listened to music on audio cassettes and vinyl records. Fascinated by beat machines, Burlesque of North America created a nostalgic screenprint of vintage music players alongside new devices, both of which are used by DJs and music enthusiasts today.

Cheung's "17 Days of Summer" is an illustration commemorating the 2012 Olympic Games using a homogenous palette of sandy beige and competitive red.

• 17 DAYS OF SUMMER •

CATCH OF THE DAY

GONE FISHING

HOOKED ON FISHING

**JORDON CHEUNG**
*GONE FISHING & COPS & ROBBERS*
*2012*

Jordon Cheung's illustrations invite us to discover stories and worlds through stylized yet detailed images. The longer we look at a print, the more we see. The prints include humorous lists of equipment that you may need when breaking into a house or going fishing. While the individual items on "Cops & Robbers" are cleverly brought together by the centered ampersand, the common thread in "Gone Fishing" is simply the fun-loving title of the print itself.

# 50 YEARS 50 TOYS

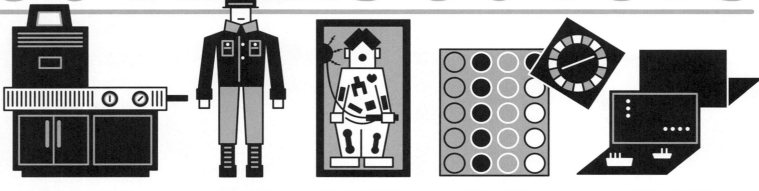

· 1963 EASY-BAKE OVEN ·

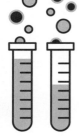
· 1964 G.I. JOE ·

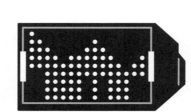
· 1965 OPERATION ·

· 1966 TWISTER ·

· 1967 BATTLESHIP ·

· 1968 HOT WHEELS ·

· 1969 CHEMISTRY SET ·

· 1970 LITE-BRIGHT ·

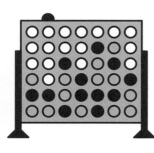
· 1971 SPACE HOPPERS ·

· 1972 UNO ·

· 1973 WALKIE TALKIE SETS ·

· 1974 TONKA TOYS TRUCKS ·

· 1975 PET ROCK ·

· 1976 CONNECT 4 ·

· 1977 "STAR WARS" FIGURES ·

· 1978 SIMON ·

· 1979 ATARI ·

· 1980 RUBIK'S CUBE ·

· 1981 LEGO TRAIN ·

· 1982 BMX BIKES ·

· 1983 CABBAGE PATCH KIDS ·

· 1984 TRANSFORMERS ·

· 1985 NINTENDO ·

· 1986 LASER TAG ·

· 1987 JENGA ·

· 1988 STARTING LINEUP · · 1989 GAME BOY · · 1990 TEENAGE MUTANT NINJA TURTLES · · 1991 SUPER NINTENDO · · 1992 BARBIE DREAM HOUSE ·

· 1993 TALKBOY · · 1994 POWER RANGERS · · 1995 BEANIE BABY · · 1996 TICKLE ME ELMO · · 1997 TAMAGOTCHI ·

· 1998 FURBY · · 1999 POKEMON · · 2000 RAZOR SCOOTER · · 2001 POGO STICK · · 2002 FURREAL CAT ·

· 2003 ROBOSAPIENS · · 2004 NINTENDO DS · · 2005 XBOX 360 · · 2006 PLAYSTATION 3 · · 2007 IPOD TOUCH ·

· 2008 NINTENDO WII · · 2009 ZHU ZHU PETS · · 2010 IPAD · · 2011 LEAPPAD · · 2012 WII U ·

# HAPPY HOLIDAYS 2013

ABBY RYAN DESIGN

ABBY RYAN DESIGN
*50 YEARS 50 TOYS, 2013*

"50 Years 50 Toys" is an illustrative infographic that reviews some of the most popular holiday toys sold in the last half-century. The two-color screen-print poster shows how the toys have shifted from simple, affordable dolls and games to mostly expensive electronics.

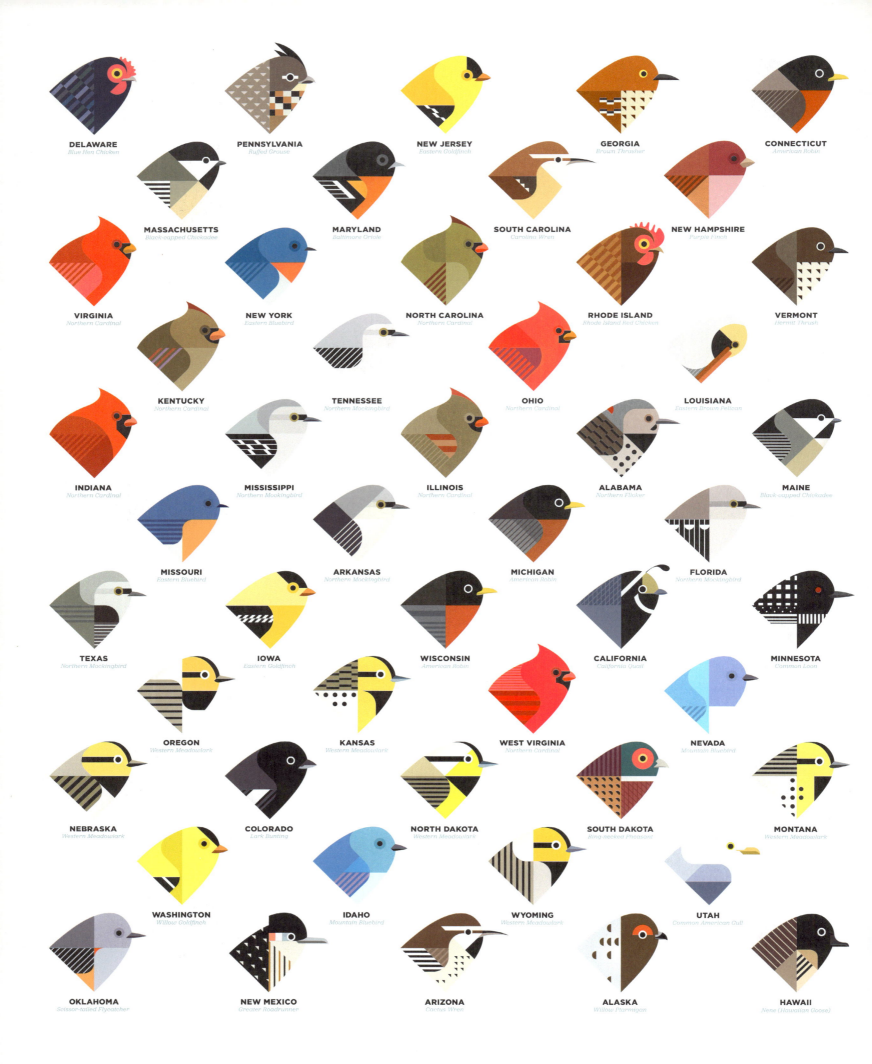

**DELAWARE**
*Blue Hen Chicken*

**PENNSYLVANIA**
*Ruffed Grouse*

**NEW JERSEY**
*Eastern Goldfinch*

**GEORGIA**
*Brown Thrasher*

**CONNECTICUT**
*American Robin*

**MASSACHUSETTS**
*Black-capped Chickadee*

**MARYLAND**
*Baltimore Oriole*

**SOUTH CAROLINA**
*Carolina Wren*

**NEW HAMPSHIRE**
*Purple Finch*

**VIRGINIA**
*Northern Cardinal*

**NEW YORK**
*Eastern Bluebird*

**NORTH CAROLINA**
*Northern Cardinal*

**RHODE ISLAND**
*Rhode Island Red Chicken*

**VERMONT**
*Hermit Thrush*

**KENTUCKY**
*Northern Cardinal*

**TENNESSEE**
*Northern Mockingbird*

**OHIO**
*Northern Cardinal*

**LOUISIANA**
*Eastern Brown Pelican*

**INDIANA**
*Northern Cardinal*

**MISSISSIPPI**
*Northern Mockingbird*

**ILLINOIS**
*Northern Cardinal*

**ALABAMA**
*Northern Flicker*

**MAINE**
*Black-capped Chickadee*

**MISSOURI**
*Eastern Bluebird*

**ARKANSAS**
*Northern Mockingbird*

**MICHIGAN**
*American Robin*

**FLORIDA**
*Northern Mockingbird*

**TEXAS**
*Northern Mockingbird*

**IOWA**
*Eastern Goldfinch*

**WISCONSIN**
*American Robin*

**CALIFORNIA**
*California Quail*

**MINNESOTA**
*Common Loon*

**OREGON**
*Western Meadowlark*

**KANSAS**
*Western Meadowlark*

**WEST VIRGINIA**
*Northern Cardinal*

**NEVADA**
*Mountain Bluebird*

**NEBRASKA**
*Western Meadowlark*

**COLORADO**
*Lark Bunting*

**NORTH DAKOTA**
*Western Meadowlark*

**SOUTH DAKOTA**
*Ring-necked Pheasant*

**MONTANA**
*Western Meadowlark*

**WASHINGTON**
*Willow Goldfinch*

**IDAHO**
*Mountain Bluebird*

**WYOMING**
*Western Meadowlark*

**UTAH**
*Common American Gull*

**OKLAHOMA**
*Scissor-tailed Flycatcher*

**NEW MEXICO**
*Greater Roadrunner*

**ARIZONA**
*Cactus Wren*

**ALASKA**
*Willow Ptarmigan*

**HAWAII**
*Nene (Hawaiian Goose)*

# STATE BIRDS

TERMINATOR

DR. STRANGELOVE

ANNIE HALL

EASY RIDER

THE INVISIBLE MAN

THE HANGOVER

LOLITA

RISKY BUSINESS, THE BLUES BROTHERS,
THE BREAKFAST CLUB, EASY A,
FERRIS BUELLER'S DAY OFF, ETC.

THE MATRIX

BIG TROUBLE IN LITTLE CHINA

X-MEN: THE LAST STAND

BILL & TED'S EXCELLENT ADVENTURE

TRUE ROMANCE

THE BIG LEBOWSKI

BACK TO THE FUTURE PART II

BREAKFAST AT TIFFANY'S

NATURAL BORN KILLERS

THELMA & LOUISE

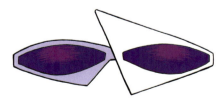

MANNEQUIN

LÉON: THE PROFESSIONAL

THEY LIVE

**GREG HARRISON**
*STATE BIRDS, 2013*

The fifty state birds of the United States are arranged here using the same pattern as the stars on the nation's flag (albeit flipped vertically to better function as a poster design). Like the stars, the birds are ordered by their respective states' admittance into the Union. The first state, Delaware, occupies the top left spot, and the fiftieth and final state, Hawaii, occupies the lower right spot.

**POST TYPOGRAPHY**
*SUMMER MOVIES, 2011*

Red heart-shaped glasses can only bring one thing to mind: sassy little Lolita. And yellow tinted Vuarnet 003s? The Big Lebowski, of course! For the New York Times's summer movies preview back in 2011, Post Typography illustrated this selection of sunglasses that have become iconic through their appearances in unforgettable films.

**TIM GEORGE**
*LIFE'S BETTER ON TWO WHEELS, 2013*

This illustration documents various kinds of motorcycles. Designer Tim George explains, "The subjects were illustrated in a very flat and observational style, each presented from the same angle and each to scale."

**CHRISTINE BERRIE**
*TUK-TUKS & JEEPNEYS, 2012/2013*
*16 RADIOS & 19 CAMERAS, 2011/2012*
*24 TELEPHONES & MICROCARS, 2010/2009*

United Airlines' **Hemispheres** magazine commissioned these illustrations for their regular feature "Three Perfect Days" on long weekend getaways. Every month, a collection of items that relate to the new destination is drawn. On the right, the drawings are of jeepneys found in Manila, and on the left Christine Berrie has illustrated a selection of tuk-tuks found in Delhi. In the simple yet detailed hand-drawn style that Berrie is known for, the prints on the following pages present a selection of transistor radios, old-fashioned cameras, old-school telephones, and microcars.

 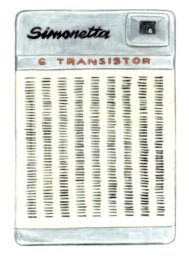  

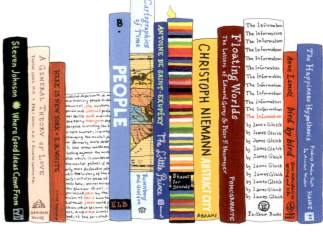

# JANE MOUNT
*THE IDEAL BOOKSHELF, 2007-ONGOING*

Jane Mount started the "Ideal Bookshelf" project in 2007 when she became fascinated by how lovely book spines look together and how in love people are with their favorite books. To date, she has painted over 800 portraits of the sets that have changed people's lives, that define them, and that they read again and again. One edition she has had to illustrate countless times is the classic Italian cookbook **The Silver Spoon.** Nevertheless, the California-based artist and illustrator will continue working on this project until she has done at least one thousand drawings of book gatherings–even if she has to illustrate **The Silver Spoon** another hundred times.

SUNGLASSES : TAKE TWO

Walgreens
SUNGLASSES

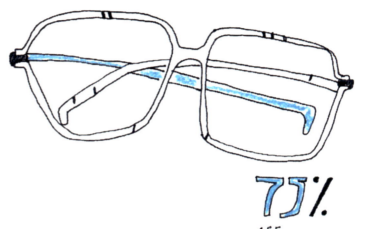

75%
OFF

i just sat on these

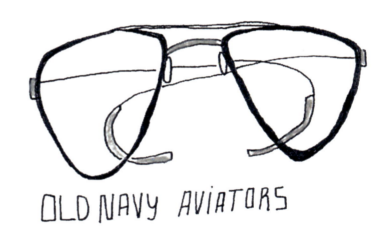

OLD NAVY AVIATORS

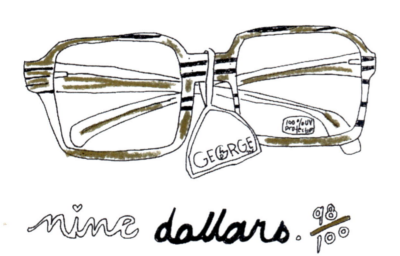

GEORGE

nine dollars. 98/100

I HAVE A PROBLEM

**KATE BINGAMAN-BURT**
*I BOUGHT ALL OF THESE, 2007*     Kate Bingaman-Burt has here compiled all the pairs of sunglasses she bought in 2006.

**CHRISTINE BERRIE**
*12 Bicycles, 2011*

"12 Bicycles" was created as a limited edition print for 20x200, a website that is dedicated to selling the works of both established and emerging artists and that encourages everyone to be an art collector.

PEUGEOT D3A - 1952
CAMION BALAI - BROOM WAGON

VOLVO 244 - 1975
TEAM MOLTENI

BUICK ELECTRA STATION WAGON - 1984
CAMPAGNOLO SERVICE OLYMPIC GAMES

SIMCA OCEANE CABRIOLET - 1958
SERVICE SANITAIRE

MERCEDES 123 - 1983
TEAM RALEIGH TI

ALPHA ROMEO 1900 - 1954
TEAM BIANCHI

PEUGEOT 403 - 1960
TEAM ST. RAPHAEL

BIANCHI S9 - 1934
RACE OFFICIALS

CITROEN CX - 1992
TEAM CARRERA JEANS

JEEP WILLYS - 1951
TOUR DE FRANCE ASSISTANCE

FIAT 600 MULTIPLA - 1960
RADIOTELEVISIONE ITALIANA

PEUGEOT 504 - 1973
MAVIC NEUTRAL SERVICE

RENAULT DAUPHINE - 1959
TEAM FRANCE ASSISTANCE

# BICYCLES

EDDY MERCKX MOTOROLA

EDDY MERCKX CLASSIC

COLNAGO MASTER

CONDOR CLASSIC

BIANCH SPECIALISSIMA

PINARELLO TEAM SKY

CERVELO CARBON

CINELLI BARRY MCGEE

GIANT COMPACT

STREET FIXED-GEAR

CURVY LO-PRO

FLYING GATE

PENNY FARTHING

PARIS GALIBIER

TANDEM

BROMPTON

BEACH CRUISER

MOTOBECANE MIXTE

## DAVID SPARSHOTT
*BICYCLE RACE SUPPORT VEHICLES & BICYCLES, 2013*

Reportage and observational drawing form an integral part of David Sparshott's practice. The illustrations "Bicycle Race Support Vehicles" and "Bicycles" were originally commissioned for the book **Bike Watching: The Explorer's Journal.** The charts were developed by researching famous bicycles known for their innovation, racing pedigree, or importance to the sport. To create his playful and detailed line-work, Sparshott uses the traditional media of graphite and colored pencils.

1930 URUGUAY
URUGUAY 4 - 2 ARGENTINA

1934 ITALY
ITALY 2 - 1 CZECHOSLOVAKIA
AET

1938 FRANCE
ITALY 4 - 2 HUNGARY

1950 BRAZIL
URUGUAY 2 - 1 BRAZIL
NO OFFICIAL FINAL

1954 SWITZERLAND
WEST GERMANY 3 - 2 HUNGARY

1958 SWEDEN
BRAZIL 5 - 2 SWEDEN

1962 CHILE
BRAZIL 3 - 1 CZECHOSLOVAKIA

1966 ENGLAND
ENGLAND 4 - 2 WEST GERMANY
AET

1970 MEXICO
BRAZIL 4 - 1 ITALY

JULES RIMET TROPHY
1930 - 1970

1974 WEST GERMANY
WEST GERMANY 2 - 1 NETHERLANDS

FIFA WORLD CUP TROPHY
1974 - PRESENT

1978 ARGENTINA
ARGENTINA 3 - 1 NETHERLANDS
AET

1982 SPAIN
ITALY 3 - 1 WEST GERMANY

1986 MEXICO
ARGENTINA 3 - 2 WEST GERMANY

1990 ITALY
WEST GERMANY 1 - 0 ARGENTINA

1994 USA
BRAZIL 0 - 0 ITALY
3 - 2 P

1998 FRANCE
FRANCE 3 - 0 BRAZIL

2002 S.KOREA + JAPAN
BRAZIL 2 - 0 GERMANY

2006 GERMANY
ITALY 1 - 1 FRANCE
5 - 3 P

2010 SOUTH AFRICA
SPAIN 1 - 0 NETHERLANDS
AET

WORLD CHAMPION

MAILLOT JAUNE

MAILLOT VERT

POLKA DOT JERSEY

MAGLIA ROSA

BIANCHI

BROOKLYN

FAEMA

MERCIER

FLANDRIA

St. RAPHAËL

MOLTENI

TI-RALEIGH

TEAM BIC

PEUGEOT

RENAULT

LA VIE CLAIRE

MAPEI

'Z' TEAM

## DAVID SPARSHOTT
*FIFA WORLD CUP WINNERS & CYCLING JERSEYS, 2013*

These images immediately bring back memories either for football fans who remember how old they were and what they were doing at the time of the World Cups or for those who won't miss a season of the legendary Tour de France. Created by David Sparshott, the first print shows the shirts worn in the final by each World Cup winner, and the second print is a chronological illustration of iconic cycle racing team jerseys that was published in the book Bike Watching: The Explorer's Journal.

HANNA MELIN
COLLECTION OF TRAINERS & LONDON
WILDLIFE, 2013/2014

Urban life can be pretty grey or to the contrary very playful and full of bright warm colors, as Hanna Melin imagines it. Intrigued by gathered objects like colorful trainers and butterflies which bring joy into a big city, the posters reflect the illustrator's observations of everyday life. When Melin noticed the countless shoe shops selling trainers in London, she started thinking of her own collection. "Collection of Trainers" shows only 1980s classics and shoes that she wore as a kid, and the colorful butterfly print is an ode to a small insect that enhances every manmade area with its fragile appearance.

LONDON WILDLIFE

**KYLER MARTZ**
*BUTTERFLIES, 2013*

These prints of butterfly designs hang near the illustrator's tattoo station and are inspired by old naturalist engravings. The Seattle-based artist combines old-school tattoos with stylized patterns depicting circus scenes, burlesque dancers, skulls, and mythical creatures. Kyler Martz arranged as many designs as could fit on these silkscreen prints for everyday inspiration.

**PENELOPE KENNY**
*THE TRANSGENIC CABINET & INSECTAFLO-RA. 2012/2013*

As genetic engineering has opened up new ways for humans to study animals, scientific findings continue to blur the division between man and other animals, thus encouraging a discourse on their similarities. Both drawings show curious entomological collections of transformed hybrid birds, moths, butterflies, and bugs. While "The Transgenic Cabinet" serves as a metaphor for our contemporary collective attitude towards trying to control, represent, and classify nature, "Insectaflora" illustrates a more harmonious model of evolutionary influence among species.

AN ILLUSTRATED GUIDE
TO BRITISH BIRDS

## CHRYSA KOUKOURA

*AN ILLUSTRATED GUIDE TO BRITISH BIRDS
& WINGED TERRESTRIAL ARTHROPODS,
2010/2010*

A fine black pen on white paper is all that Chrysa Koukoura needs in order to create vividly detailed illustrations. Here, the artist shares her favorite British birds and winged arthropods.

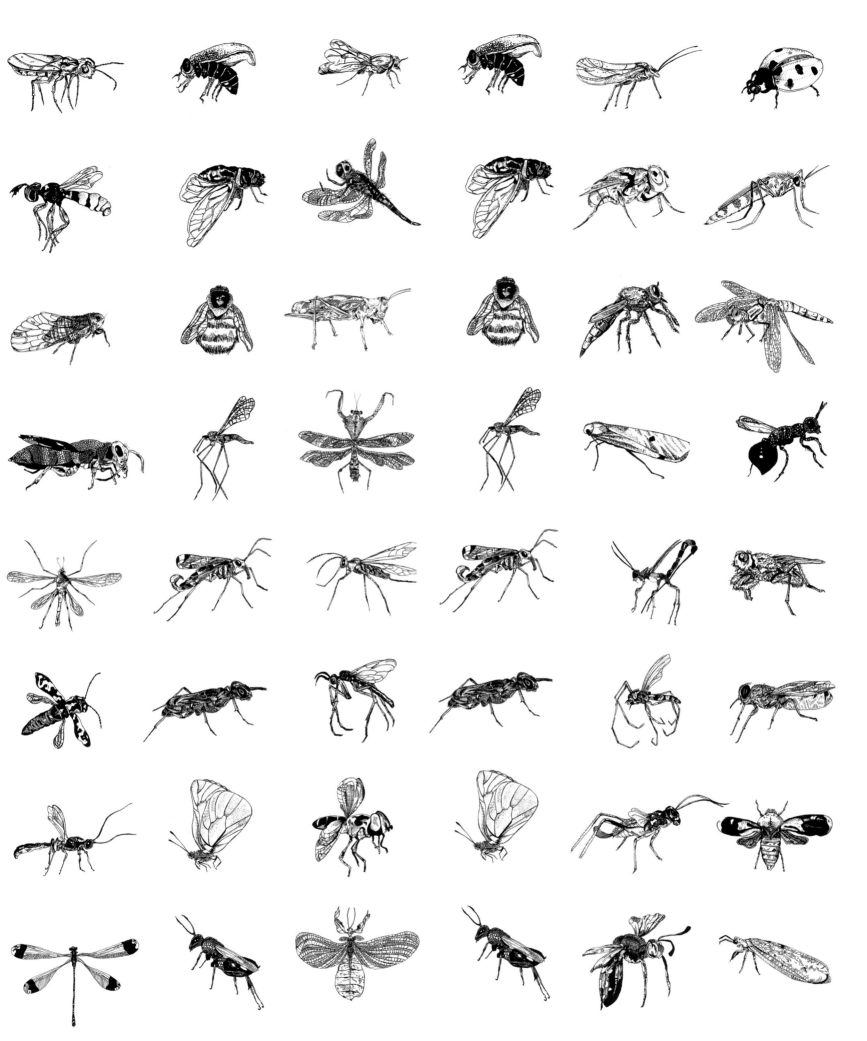

*Winged Terrestrial Arthropods*

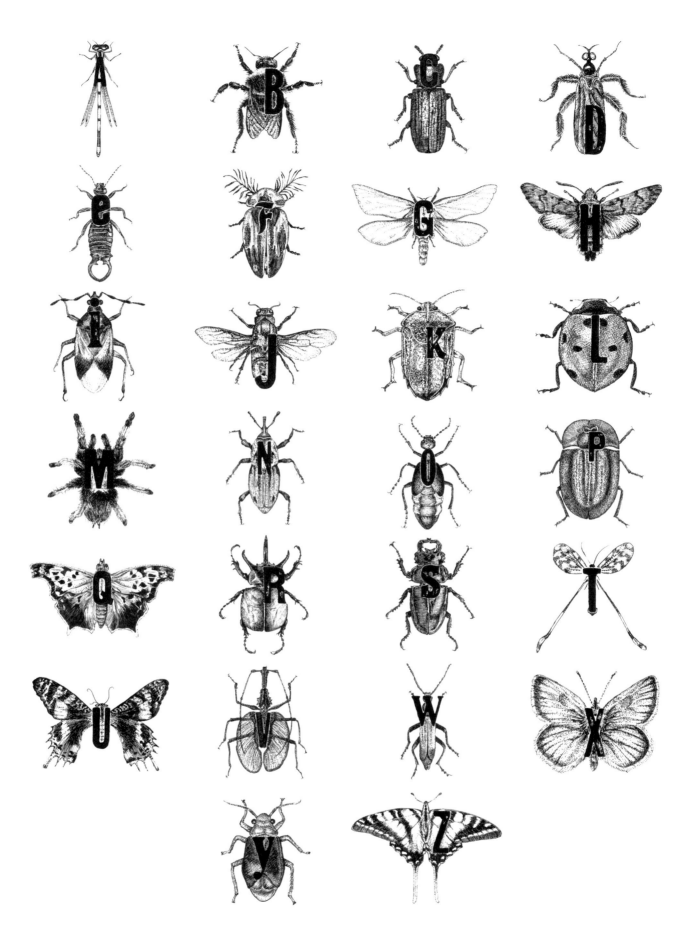

**LUCY EVES**
*ARTHROPODZ, 2014*

This entomological alphabet combines pen-and-ink illustrations with hand-printed wooden letterpress blocks to inform the viewer of each insect's initial letter. Lucy Eves's aim was to categorize a selected group of bugs and butterflies according to how their pattern or shape relates to each letterform. The final presentation of the alphabet draws inspiration from Victorian natural history compendium bookplates, with a table referencing each letter and insect at the foot of the image.

**STUDIO FM MILANO**
*TYPOGRAPHIC ENTOMOLOGY, 2010*

One has to look very closely to see that these bugs are not ordinary. For this print, typefaces are used to reproduce corresponding insects. As a butterfly and a grasshopper have very different appearances, each font is chosen carefully to maintain the insect's typology. The insect drawings were neatly arranged according to a regular grid, as if they were in a glass case at a museum of natural science. The poster further shows all individual names or scientific classifications in Latin, to which the name of the typeface used was then added.

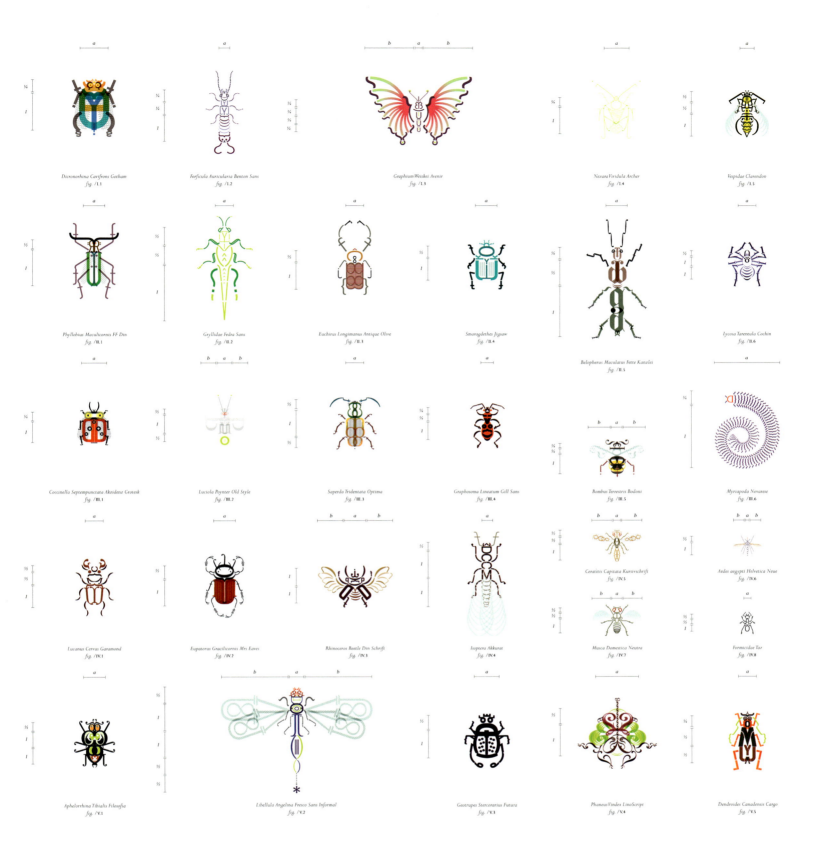

# Typographic Entomology

*Dicronorhina Carifrons Gotham* — fig. /I.1
*Forficula Auricularia Benton Sans* — fig. /I.2
*Graphium Weiskei Avenir* — fig. /I.3
*Nezara Viridula Archer* — fig. /I.4
*Vespidae Clarendon* — fig. /I.5

*Phyllobius Maculicornis FF Din* — fig. /II.1
*Gryllidae Fedra Sans* — fig. /II.2
*Euchiras Longimanus Antique Olive* — fig. /II.3
*Smaragdethes Jigsaw* — fig. /II.4
*Belopherus Maculatus Fette Kanzlei* — fig. /II.5
*Lycosa Tarentula Cochin* — fig. /II.6

*Coccinella Septempunctata Akzidenz Grotesk* — fig. /III.1
*Luciola Poynter Old Style* — fig. /III.2
*Saperda Tridentata Optima* — fig. /III.3
*Graphosoma Lineatum Gill Sans* — fig. /III.4
*Bombus Terrestris Bodoni* — fig. /III.5
*Myriapoda Novarese* — fig. /III.6

*Lucanus Cervus Garamond* — fig. /IV.1
*Eupatorus Gracilicornis Mrs Eaves* — fig. /IV.2
*Rhinoceros Beetle Din Schrift* — fig. /IV.3
*Iseptera Akkurat* — fig. /IV.4
*Ceratitis Capitata Kursivschrift* — fig. /IV.5
*Aedes aegypti Helvetica Neue* — fig. /IV.6
*Musca Domestica Neutra* — fig. /IV.7
*Formicidae Taz* — fig. /IV.8

*Aphelorrhina Tibialis Filosofia* — fig. /V.1
*Libellula Angelina Fresco Sans Informal* — fig. /V.2
*Geotrupes Stercorarius Futura* — fig. /V.3
*Phaneus Vindex LinoScript* — fig. /V.4
*Dendroides Canadensis Cargo* — fig. /V.5

## Ⓕ Ⓜ

**Entomology** (from Greek ἔντομος, entomos, "that which is cut in pieces or engraved/segmented", hence "insect"; and -λογία, -logia) is the scientific study of insects, a branch of arthropodology.
At some 1.3 million described species, insects account for more than two-thirds of all known organisms, date back some 400 million years, and have many kinds of interactions with humans and other forms of life on earth.
It is a specialty within the field of biology.
Like several of the other fields that are categorized within zoology, entomology is a taxon-based category; any form of scientific study in which there is a focus on insect related inquiries is, by definition, entomology.
Entomology therefore includes a cross section of topicsas diverse as molecular genetics, behavior, biomechanics, biochemistry, systematics, physiology, developmental biology, ecology, morphology, paleontology, anthropology, robotics, agriculture, nutrition, forensic science and more.

*from Wikipedia, the free encyclopedia*

# Dogs Of London

**Knightsbridge**
*SW1*

**Islington**
*N1*

**Blackheath**
*SE3*

**Peckham**
*SE15*

**West Ham**
*E15*

**Hackney**
*E8*

**Belgravia**
*SW1*

**East Dulwich**
*SE22*

**Walthamstow**
*E17*

**Clapham**
*SW4*

**Notting Hill**
*W11*

**Chelsea**
*SW3*

**Shoreditch**
*N1*

**Hampstead**
*NW3*

**Muswell Hill**
*N10*

**Richmond**
*SW14*

ANNA WALSH
*DOGS OF LONDON, 2008*

A beautifully drawn collection of dogs you might run into in London, depending on whether you are walking through charming Chelsea or hip Hampstead.

ROBIN

TUI

WEKA

KAKA

NATIVE PIGEON

BLACK OYSTER CATCHER

KEA

TOMTIT

KIWI

KINGFISHER

FANTAIL

TAKAHE

KATE SUTTON

*BIRDS OF NEW ZEALAND, 2013*

Kate Sutton's work is heavily influenced by nature. "I am at my happiest in the countryside or by the sea," she explains. This charming illustration assembles some of New Zealand's birds with the whimsical touch that Sutton is famous for.

NUTMEG
MUNIA

YELLOW
WAGTAIL

FAIRY
MARTIN

SCARLET
ROBIN

ZEBRA
FINCH

HOUSE
SPARROW

CITRINE
WAGTAIL

WELCOME
SWALLOW

YELLOW
ROBIN

EASTERN
WHIPBIRD

BIRDS
OF
AUSTRALIA

GREY
FANTAIL

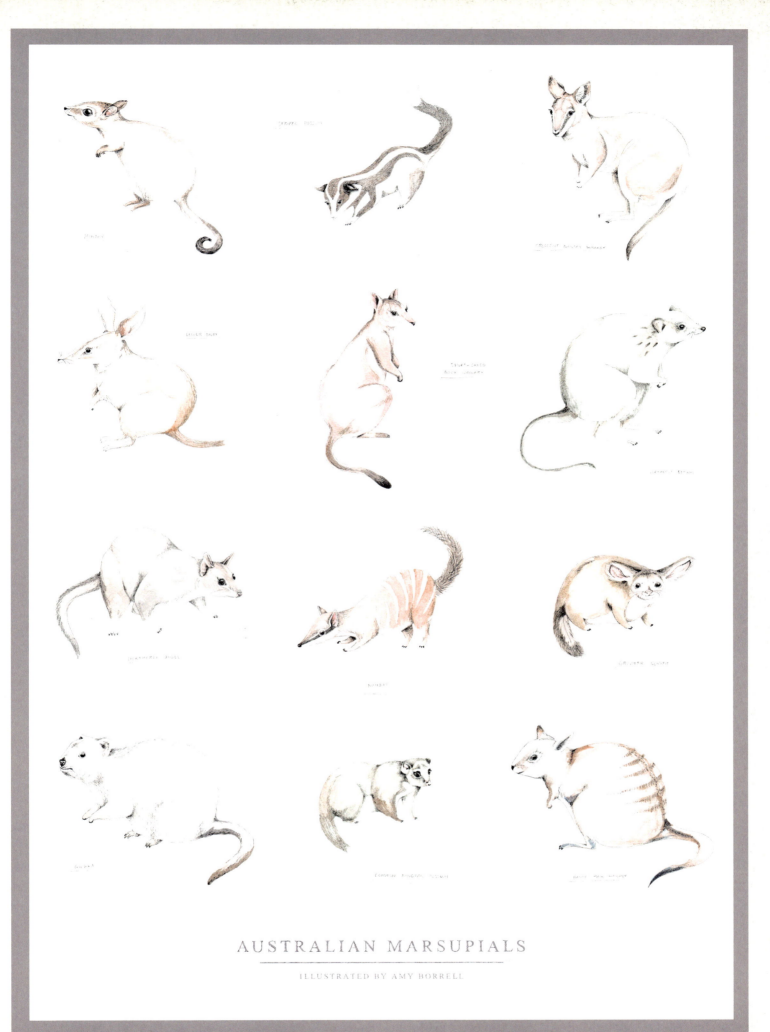

# AUSTRALIAN MARSUPIALS

ILLUSTRATED BY AMY BORRELL

# The
# OWL FACTOR
## a collection of owl voices

**MEGASCOPS TRICHOPSIS**

(Whiskered Screech Owl)

" *hu-hu-hu-hu-hu-hu-hu,
..........hu-hu-hu-hu-hu-hu* "

**TYTO SOUMAGNEI**

(Madagascar Red Owl)

" *wac-wac-wac...........and
another single, explosive call* "

**PSEUDOSCOPS GRAMMICUS**

(Jamaican Owl)

"......*a curious 'wow' and a
tremulous 'whoooooo'*......"

**STRIX URALENSIS**

(Ural Owl)

" *hohohohohohohuhuho,..........
hohohohohohohuhuho,..........* "

**PTILOPSIS LEUCOTIS**

(White-faced Screech Owl)

" *w-h-h-h-h-h-h-oo,..........
w-h-h-h-h-h-h-oo,...........* "

**GLAUCIDIUM SJOSTEDTI**

(Sjöstedt's Owlet)

" *pürr pürr pürr-
pürr-pürr-pürr* "

**STRIX ALUCO**

(Tawny Owl)

" *hüüüüw....................
hü hühühü..................* "

**BUBO SCANDIACUS**

(Snowy Owl)

" *krow-ow.......krow-ow
...........rick-rick-rick.* "

**GLAUCIDIUM PERLATUM**

(Pearl Spotted Owl)

" *hu hu hü hü hee hee
heeew heeew heeew, ...* "

**STRIX NEBULOSA**

(Great Grey Owl)

" *hoo hoo hoo hoo
hoo hoo hoo hoo* "

**STRIX VIRGATA**

(Mottled Owl)

" *bo bo bo bo bo bo bo bo bo bo
bo bo bo-bo-bobo,...........* "

**ASIO OTUS**

(Long-eared Owl)

" *oo....oo....oo....oo....oo....
oo....oo....oo....oo....oo....* "

**BUBO BUBO**

(Eurasian Eagle Owl)

" *ho ho ho-ho-ho huuhoo............
ho ho ho-ho-ho huuhoo............* "

**Garudio Studiage**

ANNA WALSH

*THE OWL FACTOR & BUDGET BUDGIES
2014/2013*

The world of birds is magical yet bizarre. Inspired by Paris-based Deyrolle natural history information posters, the illustrated print "The Owl Factor" shows that owl voices are much more varied than a simple "who who" sound. Or take the cutthroat world of budgerigar shows: "Budget Budgies" celebrates the weird world of champion budgerigar breeding and gives it a high-street twist by spotting the similarities between pet competitions and budget high-street shops. While budgie owners obsess over pedigrees, colors, and fanciful names, high-street shops battle to grab our attention with bright logos and catchy slogans.

# Budget Budgies

*cheap cheap cheap*

Argos
Avante-garde

Asda's Pride &
Lidl Love

Easyjet Joy &
Ryan's Airhead

Poundland
Princess

Cash Converter's
Casuist

Iceland's Idyll &
Iceland's Illuminati

Travel Lodge
Treasure &
Premier Inn
Prema Donna

Primark Prince &
Tesco's Valuable

Garudio
Studiage

## JAMES BARKER

*DINOSAURS OF THE PREHISTORIC WORLD & EXTINCT ANIMALS OF THE PREHISTORIC WORLD, 2013*

Museums of natural history and **Jurassic Park** made them famous. Dinosaurs and other pre-historic creatures are intriguing because of their unusual shapes and their massive sizes. Just think of the Triceratops's head with three horns or T. rex's disproportionate arms com-pared to the rest of its body. Yet despite a substantial amount of images, nobody knows what these giants really looked like. When James Barker started to catalogue and build a collection of prehistoric creatures which have gone extinct in much more recent years or are currently facing extinction, he decided to at-tribute patterns from present-day lizards or mammals to the different types of dinosaurs he illustrated.

# MASKS OF THE WORLD

## AN EXHIBITION

AT SOME MUSEUM. BUT NOT HERE

**JAMES BARKER**
*MASKS OF THE WORLD & PLANES OF THE
SECOND WORLD WAR, 2009*

Many things that form a cohesive and engaging collection have not been shown under one roof for the purpose of an exhibition, or at least not yet. The illustrations "Masks of the World" and "Planes of the Second World War" aim to build collections of objects that James Baker found worth compiling and aesthetically appealing because of their patterns and designs. The drawings allow us to admire and compare these gatherings that only exist on paper.

RHODANTHE MANGLESII

COMESPERMA VIRGATUM

BANKSIA PRIONOTES

## AMY BORRELL
*FLORA, 2013*

Australian flora is incredibly varied and one of the country's greatest treasures, with a staggering 24,000 native plant species. Fascinated by her homeland's vegetation, Amy Borrell creates delicate pieces that reflect her rich surroundings. Frankie & Swiss, a boutique textile printing and design studio based in Melbourne that celebrates nature, commissioned this hand-painted study of Australian flora for their "Leaf Series."

BURCHARDIA UMBELLATA

EUCALYPTUS
LEUCOXYLON

TELOPEA SPECIOSISSIMA

ACTINONIUM
CUNNINGHAMII

ASTROLOMA FOLIFOLIUM

INDIGOFERA AUSTRALIS

OZOTHAMNUS SECUNDIFLORUS

*Amy Borrell*

**HANNA MELIN**
*COLLECTION OF BARRATT HOMES*
*& COLLECTION OF SUNSHINE, 2014/2010*

Intriguing patterns and interesting images emerge when one puts objects in grids. In the U.K., "Barratt Homes" are the most common houses you'll see. Their structures and designs are simple and repetitive. By drawing the slightly different types on paper, the illustrator shows an endearing appreciation for these houses, thereby making them look a little bit less ordinary. "Collection of Sunshine," on the other hand, is a decorative image that transports you to beach holidays and sticky sweet summer afternoons.

57

# STEPHEN CHEETHAM
*140 CHARACTERS, 2013*

U.K. illustration agency Handsome Frank has created an art gallery that was crowdsourced via Twitter. Entitled "Tweet-A-Brief," the exhibition sought "illustrative briefs" from Twitter users and then passed the ideas on to the artists for inspiration. Stephen Cheetham's brief was simply "140 characters," as that is the maximum length of a tweet. He did indeed illustrate 140 characters, but with a twist: each character is represented by an amusing personality with a distinctive style, thereby playing on the double meaning of the word "character." Cheetham's vector-based images combine bright colors, clean lines, and a bit of British humor here and there.

## I INFOGRAFIA

*STICKERS BOOKLET DO YOU HAVE ANY TO TRADE?, 2011*

Popular figures from Portuguese football history are illustrated here as if they were stickers. The names of the figures are purposefully not shown next to each player, inviting viewers to guess who is who.

  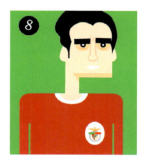  

Text: Rui Miguel Tovar

01 - ERIKSSON DE FÉRIAS, 02 - FIGO, 03 - JOSÉ AUGUSTO, 04 - BENTO, 05 - CHALANA, 06 - HUMBERTO COELHO, 07 - TONI, 08 - JOSÉ TORRES, 9 - RUI BARROS, 10 - DI STÉFANO, 11 - GERMANO, 12 - CÉSAR BRITO, 13 - BALAKOV, 14 - JORGE CORDADO, 15 - ERIKSSON NO TRABALHO, 16 - FERNANDO MARTINS, 17 - EUSEBIO, 18 - MATATEU, 19 - GUTTMANN, 20 - PEIXE, 21 - OCTAVIO MACHADO, 22 - BORGES COUTINHO, 23 - SOUSA CINTRA, 24 - NENÉ, 25 - DOMINGUEZ, 26 - STRÖMBERG, 27 - CUBILLAS 28 - JORDAO, 29 - JOSÉ ÁGUAS, 30 - PINGA, 31 - YUSTRICH, 32 - PEYROTEO, 33 - COLUNA, 34 - DAMAS, 35 - JOAO V. PINTO, 36 - MÁRIO WILSON, 37 - JORGE MENDONÇA, 38 - OTTO GLÓRIA, 39 - JOAO ALVES, 40 - VITOR BAIA, 41 - CANDIDO DE OLIVEIRA, 42 - VITOR BAPTISTA, 43 - ARTUR JORGA, 44 - PREUD'HOMME, 45 - MALCOLM ALLISON, 46 - DITO, 47 - VELOSO, 48 - YAZALDE, 49 - JARDEL, 50 - ROMEU

**HEY STUDIO**
*HEY CHRISTMAS, 2012*

As soon as Christmas time comes, people start to think about the different ways of communicating a warm and personal message to their friends, partners, and family members. Hey Studio found their own way by designing atypical Christmas cards, a method that seemed obvious to the Barcelona-based graphic design studio. Ever since then, they send out their wishes using stylized scenes of Jesus Christ's birthday, colorful Christmas trees, and sparkling stars.

**SCOTT PARK**
*SYNTHESPIANS, 2013*

What exactly is a robot? Do only purely mechanical characters qualify? What about cyborgs and artificial organisms? Soon after Scott Park started to create a poster with his favorite robots, he discovered that the term "robot" is too narrow. He came to realize that the interpretation of the idea of a robot varied as much as the films and shows that featured them. So he broadened the theme and drew 66 famous synthetic characters like robots, cyborgs, holograms, and computers from famous television shows and movies.

SYNTHESPIANS

ROBOCOP - STAR TREK: THE NEXT GENERATION - ASTRO BOY - STAR WARS: EPISODE IV, A NEW HOPE - TERMINATOR 2: JUDGEMENT DAY - THE VENTURE BROTHERS - THE SIX MILLION DOLLAR MAN - THE DAY THE EARTH STOOD STILL
BATTLESTAR GALACTICA (2004) - SILENT RUNNING - FUTURAMA - VOLTRON - MOON - STAR TREK: THE MOTION PICTURE - SPACE CAMP - WESTWORLD - TRON - DOCTOR WHO - A.I. ARTIFICIAL INTELLIGENCE - BATTLESTAR GALACTICA (1978)
TERMINATOR 2: JUDGEMENT DAY - PACIFIC RIM - THE HITCHHIKERS GUIDE TO THE GALAXY - AUSTIN POWERS: INTERNATIONAL MAN OF MYSTERY - I, ROBOT - THE MATRIX - ROBOCOP - STAR TREK: VOYAGER - 2001: A SPACE ODYSSEY - THE MUPPETS - ALIENS - SHORT CIRCUIT - SPACEBALLS
THE IRON GIANT - THE STEPFORD WIVES (1975) - ALIEN - THE BLACK HOLE - STAR WARS: THE CLONE WARS - THE BIONIC WOMAN (1976) - LOGAN'S RUN - TOTAL RECALL (1990) - BILL & TED'S BOGUS JOURNEY - KNIGHT RIDER - PROMETHEUS - ADVENTURE TIME - FARSCAPE - THX 1138
THE INCREDIBLES - BUCK ROGERS IN THE 25TH CENTURY - STAR WARS: EPISODE 1, THE PHANTOM MENACE - BLADE RUNNER - MOBILE SUIT GUNDAM - THE TRANSFORMERS (1984) - DOCTOR WHO - BATTERIES NOT INCLUDED - STAR TREK: THE NEXT GENERATION - METROPOLIS
LOST IN SPACE - TERMINATOR: THE SARAH CONNER CHRONICLES - ELYSIUM - WALL-E - RED DWARF - STAR WARS: EPISODE V, THE EMPIRE STRIKES BACK - THE JETSONS

# STAR CARS - VOL 2

BACK TO THE FUTURE II - TRANSFORMERS - FANTASY ISLAND - TORCHWOOD - VANISHING POINT (1971) - PLANES, TRAINS AND AUTOMOBILES - THUNDERBIRDS - WALLACE & GROMMIT: THE CURSE OF THE WERE-RABBIT
HARDCASTLE AND McCORMICK - KNIGHT RIDER - RISKY BUSINESS - AMERICAN GRAFFITI - THE GREEN HORNET - CHERRY 2000 - CONDORMAN - MAXIMUM OVERDRIVE - 101 DALMATIONS - DEATH PROOF - THE DUKES
OF HAZZARD - MEGAFORCE - BLACK MOON RISING - MEN IN BLACK - THE SAINT - TOMMY BOY - BREAKING BAD - STAR WARS EPISODE I: THE PHANTOM MENACE - ARCHER - THE JETSONS - XXX - THE GREAT RACE - DEATH RACE - DAZED AND CONFUSED - TERMINATOR 2: JUDGEMENT DAY
M.A.S.K. - SPACEBALLS - ROBOCOP - THE BIG LEBOWSKI - THE FLINTSTONES - GHOSTBUSTERS 2 - AUTOMAN - JOE DIRT - COBRA - THE ROCKFORD FILES - MARVEL: AGENTS OF S.H.I.E.L.D. - THX1138 - DUDE, WHERE'S MY CAR? - THE CANNONBALL RUN - THE MONKEES - GONE IN 60
SECONDS (1974) - THE AVENGERS - INSPECTOR GADGET - HAROLD AND MAUDE - STRIPES - REPO MAN - TANGO AND CASH - BACK TO THE FUTURE III - TWO-LANE BLACKTOP - HARRY POTTER AND THE PRISONER OF AZKABAN - THUNDERCATS - THE CAR - THE INCREDIBLES - THE DUEL
THE BOURNE IDENTITY - THE MUNSTERS - THE FRENCH CONNECTION - TAXI - STRANGE BREW - CAPTAIN AMERICA : THE FIRST AVENGER - DAMNATION ALLEY - LOST - THE SIMPSONS

**SCOTT PARK**
*STAR CARS VOLUME 2, 2014*

Growing up, there were two things that Scott Park loved: movies and cars. The illustrator explains, "It didn't matter if the movie was good, bad, funny, or dramatic. I always noticed the cars. What kind of car a character drives is almost never accidental. The cars are carefully cast. They become extensions of the characters, or sometimes they even become characters themselves." Park combined all of his interests in this poster by drawing cars, vans, buses, and trucks from movies he has watched.

**REMIE GEOFFROI**
*NEW YORK CITY FOOD TRUCKS, 2010*

**New York Magazine** commissioned this visual to illustrate an article on the growing popularity of specialty food trucks in New York City.

## Aircraft

### 01 × Airbus A319

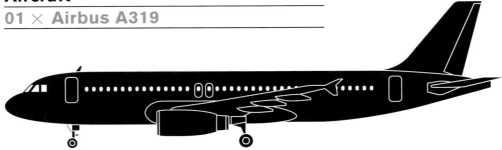

### 01 × Boeing 777

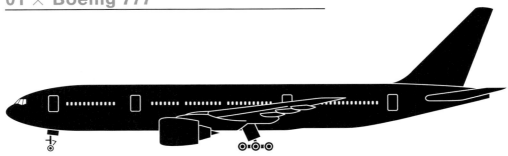

## Helicopter

### 02 × Augusta SH-3D/TS

## Car

### 01 × Mercedes-Benz ML 430

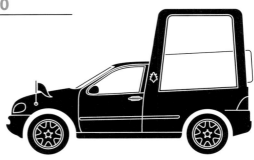

## Motorcycle

### 02 × Ducati MultistradaML 430

## Aircraft

**02 × BAE 146**

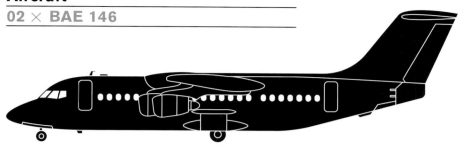

## Train

**01 × Royal Train**

## Carriages

**01 × Gold State Coach**

## Carriages

**01 × Irish State Coach**

## Cars

**02 × State Bentley Arnages**

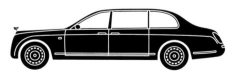

**RUSSELL BELL**
*ME AND MY MOTORCADE: MONTHLY*
*SINCE 2009*

"Me and My Motorcade" (which continues on pages 68–69), is a long-running monthly feature in **Monocle** magazine illustrating the various modes of transport available to global leaders. The ones featured on the above two pages are the motorcades of the Pope and her Majesty Queen Elizabeth II.

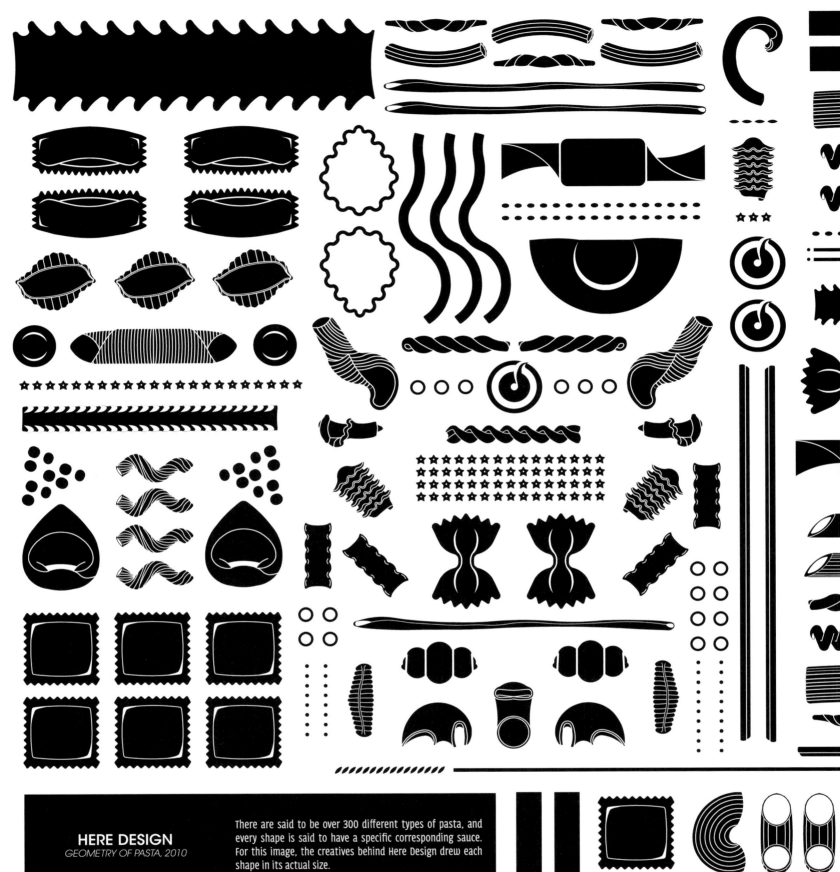

Recipes: Jacob Kenedy, Illustrations: Lisa Vandy

## HERE DESIGN
*GEOMETRY OF PASTA, 2010*

There are said to be over 300 different types of pasta, and every shape is said to have a specific corresponding sauce. For this image, the creatives behind Here Design drew each shape in its actual size.

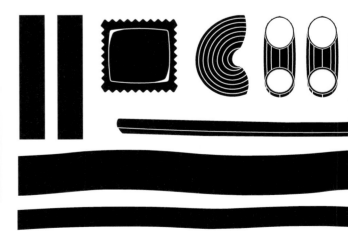

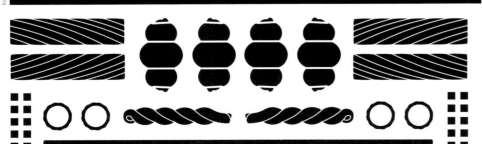

 **STL**

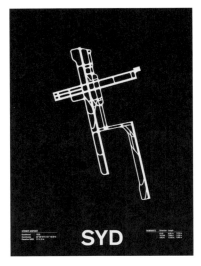 **SYD**

 **TLV**

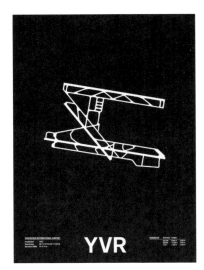 **YVR**

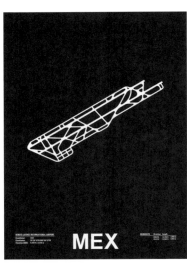 **MEX**

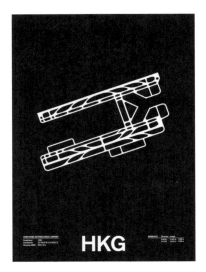 **HKG**

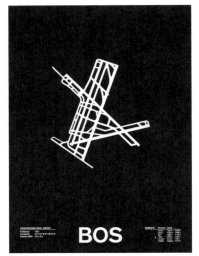 **BOS**

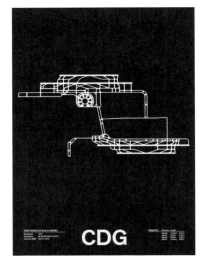 **CDG**

 **MSP**

 **MDW**

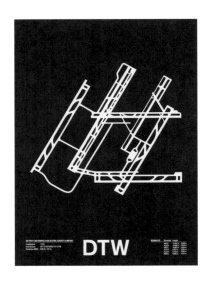 **DTW**

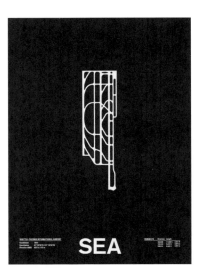 **SEA**

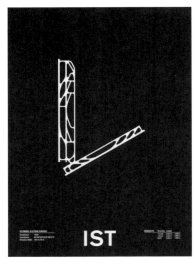 **IST**

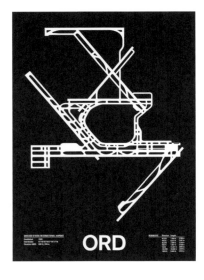 **ORD**

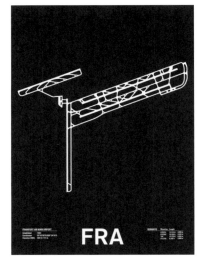 **FRA**

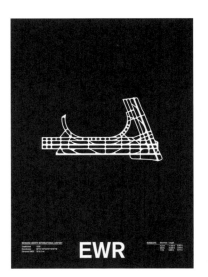 **EWR**

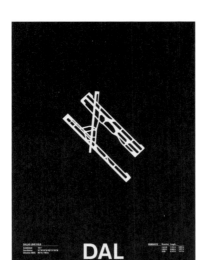

**DAL**

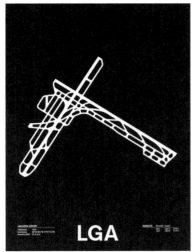

**LGA**

**SFO**

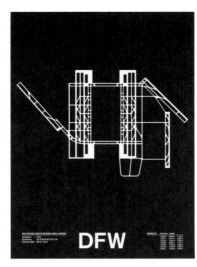

**DFW**

**CPH**

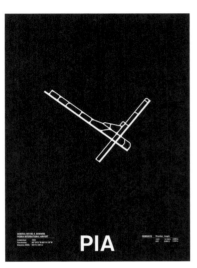

**PIA**

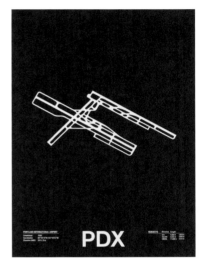

**PDX**

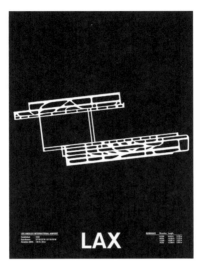

**LAX**

**SAN**

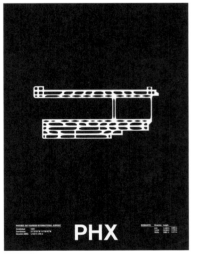

**PHX**

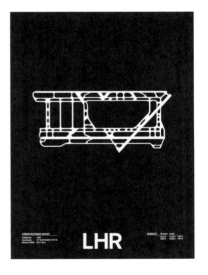

**LHR**

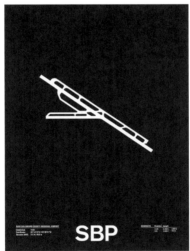

**SBP**

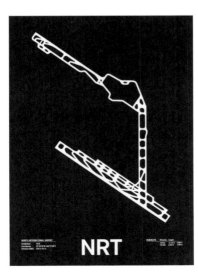

**NRT**

## NOMO DESIGN
*RUNWAY SCREEN PRINT SERIES, 2012*

NOMO Design, a.k.a. Jerome Daksiewicz, succeeded in reducing intimidating and often chaotic airport structures to visually appealing, clean designs. The print series illustrates the various layouts of airports around the world with intriguing precision, and includes each airport's three-letter IATA code as well as statistical information.

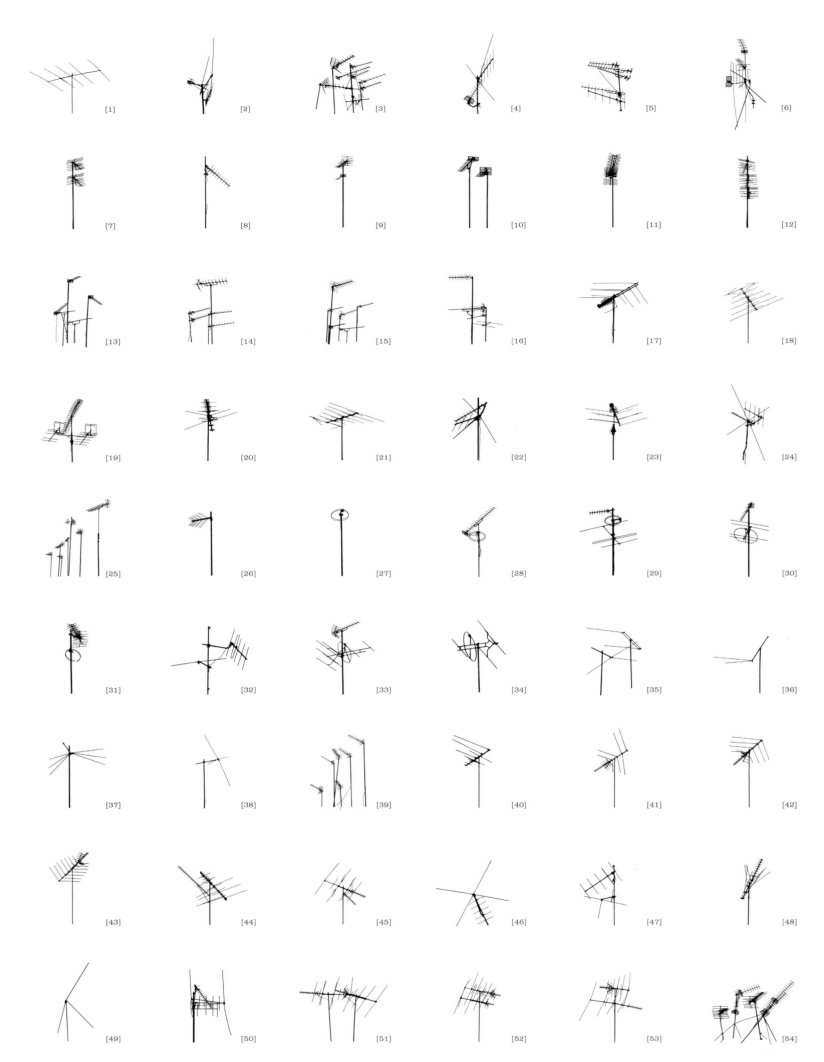

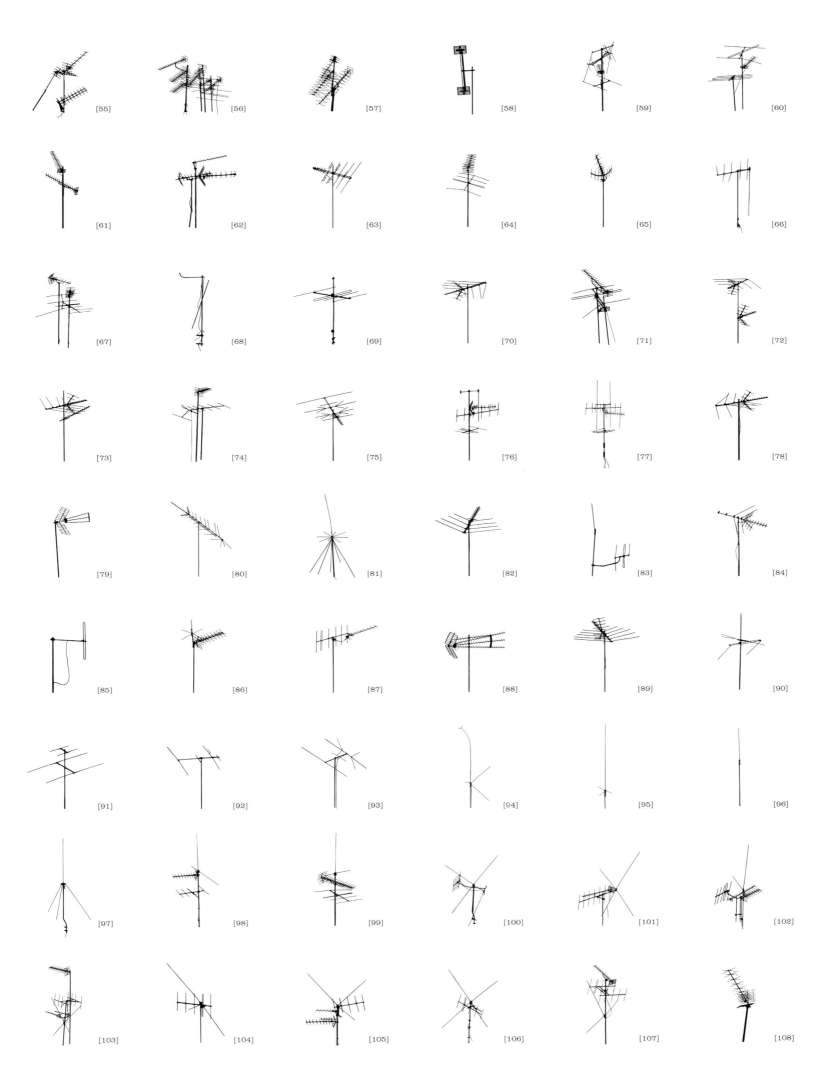

IAN MCDONNELL
*I LIKE AERIALS, 2008*

"I like Aerials" is a collection of 108 television antennae. These ubiquitous objects populate many rooftops yet are very easy to ignore. But when put into focus and presented in this visually appealing context, they disclose an unexpected beauty. These aerials are reproduced and illustrated from photographic research carried out in New York, London, Newcastle, and Cardiff.

**Holiday Essentials**

| | | | | | | | | | | |
|---|---|---|---|---|---|---|---|---|---|---|
| Fur trapper hat | Photo with Santa | Present | Fireplace channel | Partridge in a pear tree | Mrs. Claus | Log | Christmas green | Snowball | Santa Claus parade | Hot cocoa |
| Penguin | Bad gift | Santa's sack | P-a-a-r-ty | Snow | Leg warmers | Gift card | Jack Frost | Santa's snack | Candles | Earmuffs |
| Three Wise Men | Charlie Brown Christmas | Jingle bells | Elk | Yule log | Ice fishing | Pet humiliation | Candy | Hangover | Sleigh ride | Dasher |
| Chimney | Bad family portrait | Christmas tree farm | Wood chopping | Curling | Toque | | Snow angel | Eggnog | Gingerbread house | Office party |
| Mitten | Bobsled | Snowman | | Snowflake | Santa's list | Christmas | Toboggan | The Nutcracker | Holiday classic |
| Snowy owl | Test of patience | Christmas lists | Sugar Mountain | Bing Crosby album | Bare tree | Bunny hill | Prancer | Elf hat | Wreath | Flu shot |
| Awkward in-law moment | Turkey | Office party | Grinch | Snow fort | | Santa | | Christmas Past | Ghost of Christmas Present | Ghost of Christmas Yet to Come |
| Party shoes | Vixen | Church | Season | Hot Toddy | Snow boot | Runny nose | Snow day! | Christmas lights | Long johns | Snow globe |
| Hockey sticks | Candy cane | Ice sculpture | Elf shoes | Carolers | Christmas tree | Snowshoes | | | | Sled dog |
| Skates | Gift receipt | Sled | Gloves | New Year's countdown | Gingerbread woman | Ugly sweater | Igloo | Wine | Hockey puck | Comet |
| Abominable snowman | Garland | Angel | Cupid | Snowboarder | Las Posadas | Love | Snowplow | Hockey helmet | Ski boots | Canada goose |
| Nutcracker | Ski school | Ski poles | Holly | Apple cider | Inflatable Santa | Antler hat | Baby Jesus | Kwanzaa | Dreidel | Greeting card |
| Gingerbread man | Poinsettia | Winter getaway | Ski lift | Bow | Fake snow | Donner | Nativity scene | Santa's sleigh | Gift tag | Fireplace |
| Santa's beard | Iceberg | Hanukkah | Polar bear | Dancer | Stocking | Snow goggles | Cable car | Jingles | Rudolf | Pine cone |
| Log house | Blitzen | Feliz Navidad | Parka | Letter to Santa | Scrooge | Hot water bottle | Credit card | Christmas red | Tinsel | Regift |

**All that glitters is gold.**

*Ben Weeks* (signature)

## BEN WEEKS
*ALL THAT GLITTERS IS GOLD, 2011*

165 neatly presented holiday-related thoughts, memories, and objects presented in icon form by Toronto-based illustrator and designer Ben Weeks.

Art Director: Philip Pan. Paper: Mohawk Loop Antique Vellum Black 80lb. Copy Writer: Doug Dolan Design. Firm: Genesys Creative Designer: Leah Renihan Designers: Clare Chou. Printing: Somerset

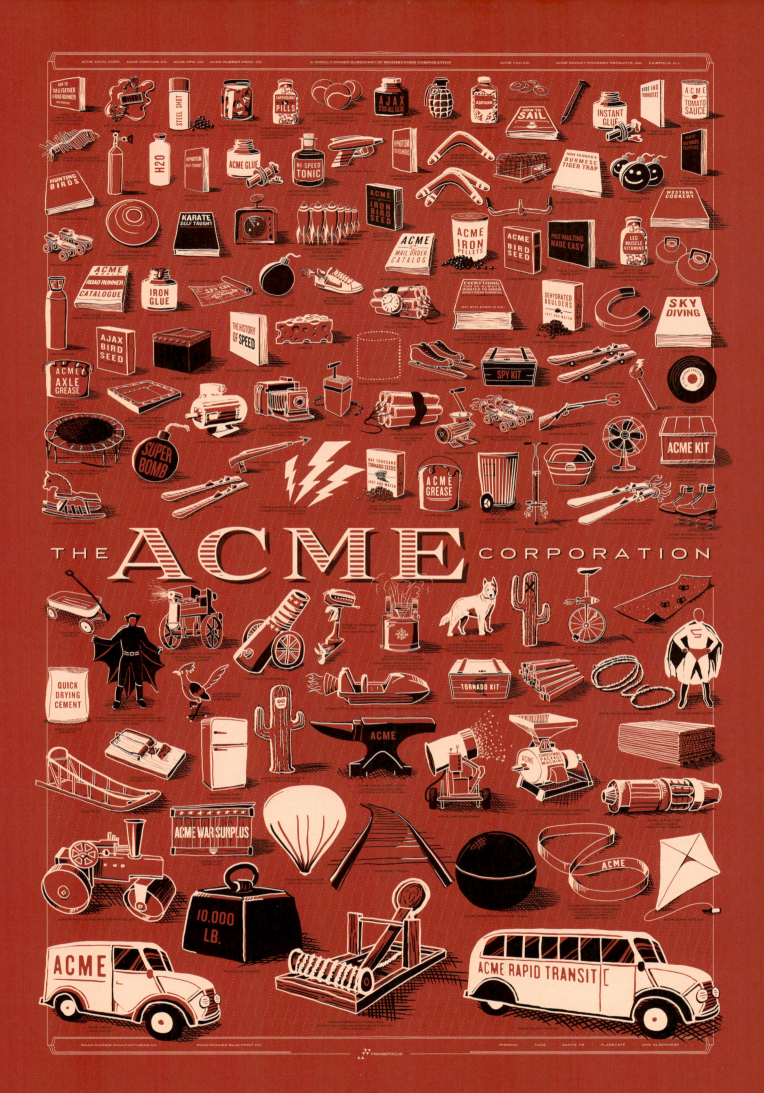

**FRINGE FOCUS**
*THE ACME CORPORATION, 2013*

Artist Rob Loukotka spent over 100 hours researching, designing, and illustrating this screen print, which features all of the outlandish products produced by the fictional ACME corporation that Wile E. Coyote used to try to catch the Road Runner in the famous cartoon. The poster includes drawings of all 126 explosives, gadgets, rockets, and more.

**BMD DESIGN**
*CAFÉ RACER 2010-2011*

French graphic design studio BMD Design has created four Café Racers using graphic techniques from the 1930s where lettering and background are one, allowing the motorcycle to stand out. Drawing and typography here elegantly interact.

**The Quiet Riot**
It was the mid-'80s. It was Chicago.
Give Jim McMahon a break.

**The Farrah Fawcett**
Joe Montana, a fluffy-haired San
Francisco treat.

**The Penitent**
A clean, post-prison look for the
Eagles' Michael Vick.

**The Vinnie Chase**
In case he keeps throwing picks, Jets QB
Mark Sanchez is Hollywood-ready.

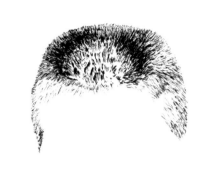

**The Pelt**
A no-nonsense 'do for a no-nonsense dude
(the Hall of Famer Johny Unitas).

**The Fourth and Long**
Tom Brady's Giselle-influenced hair
is depressing. It just is.

**The Ringo**
It is not known if the bowl has ever been
removed from Roman Gabriel's head.

**The Fade Route**
Randall Cunningham's hair could also
serve as a coaster for your drink.

**The Dazed and Confused**
Ken Stabler looks as if he wants to
take you for a ride in his van.

CHRISTINA CHRISTOFOROU
*NINE OF A KIND: QUARTERBACK HAIRCUTS
& THE BANDS HAIR PORTRAITS POSTER
2011/2007*

These two posters by Christina Christoforou are all about hair, an aspect of our physique that the illustrator considers to be "a language" in itself, as "it reveals information about our choices and our personality, and is a defining element of our perception of each other." The poster on the left compiles nine of the best worst quarterback haircuts along with ruthlessly humorous names and commentary, and on the right, the "Bands Hair Portraits Poster" invites viewers to guess who the artists are based on their hairdos.

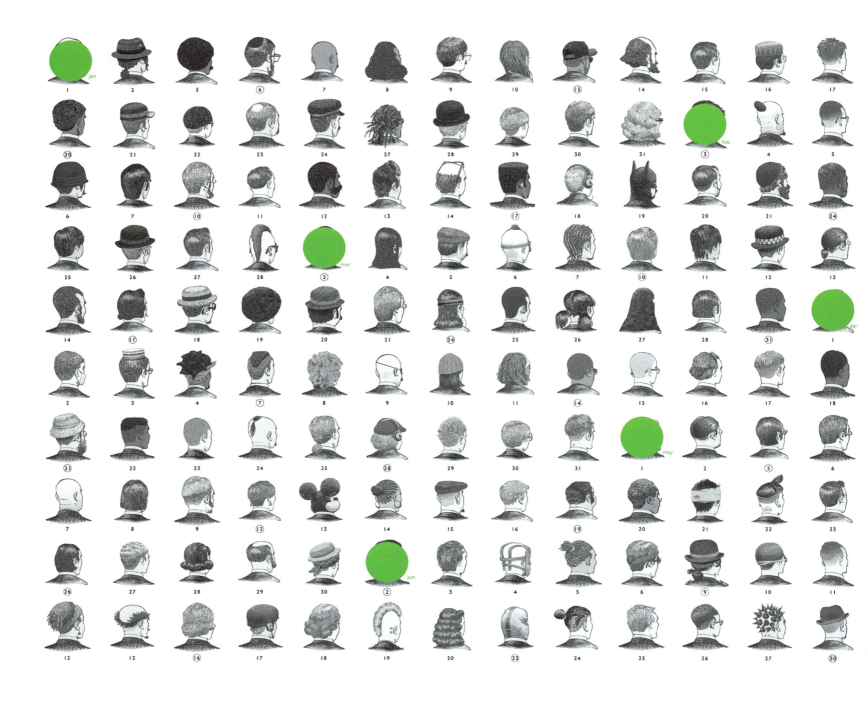

**PAGE TSOU**
*NO WEEKENDS, 2014*

In this twist on the common calendar, London-based artist Page Tsou decided to leave out weekends. He explains that while the prospect of the weekend engenders great joy, once Monday comes around people tend to be struck by a wave of depression, and "if we change our view slightly, Mondays can be like any other day."

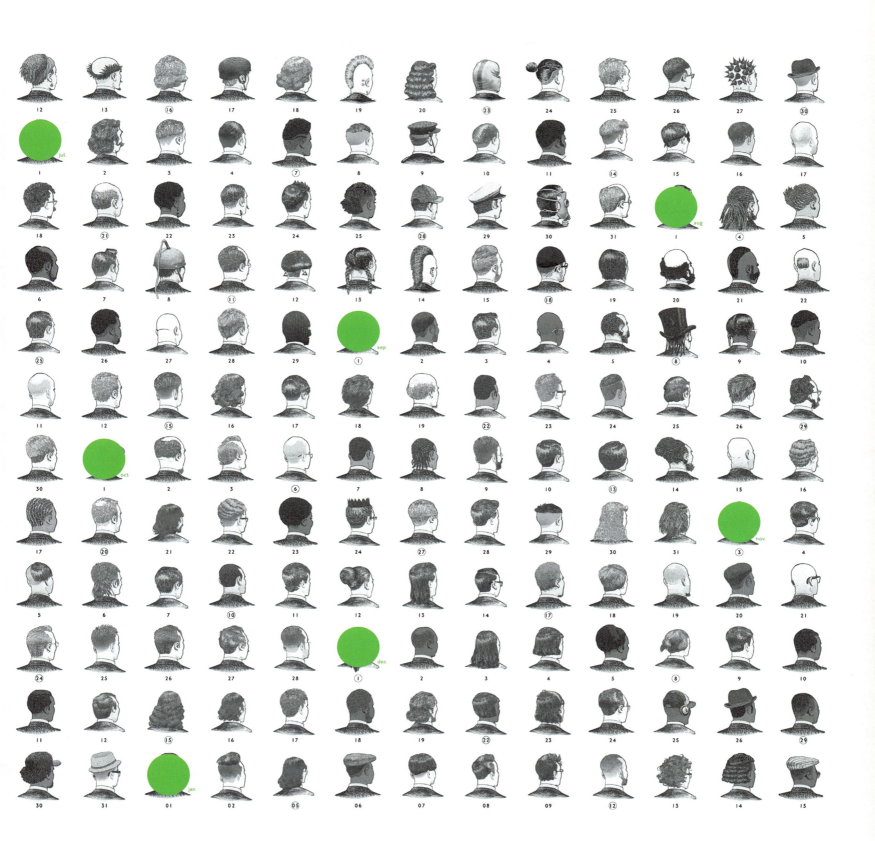

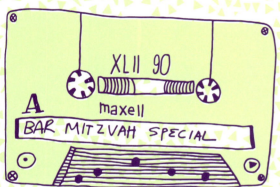

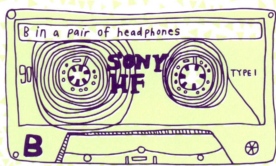

SCREW **DRIVER**

Glue Sticks.

**HAMMER**

DRILL

PEN

MOLESKINE®

Laptop

PENCIL SHARPENER.

YELLOW TWINE

Super Fancy

Union PENCIL

SEWING MACHINE

CRAFT FEATHERS

EXTRA FAT

X·ACTO

Spray Cap

PAINT BRUSHES

Pink Pearl®

ELEVEN GOOGLE EYES

GOLD STARS

SCISSORS

BOOKLET STAPLER

COLOR PENCILS

TAPE

ruler

IRON STEAMER

INDIA INK
• WATERPROOF
• DEEP OPAQUE
• CONFORMS TO ASTM
2 oz. (60 ml)

Super Glue...

SUPER GLUE Gel
.07 oz.

PROFESSIONAL

ACRYLIC SCREEN PRINTING INK

Silver

BONE FOLDER

**TOOLS FOR MAKING.**

three yellow legal pads

**KATE BINGAMAN-BURT**
*OTHER PEOPLE'S MIXTAPES & TOOLS FOR MAKING, 2010–2013/2008–2014*

After struggling to find mixtapes in thrift shops and second-hand stores, Kate Bingaman-Burt posted an open call on the internet for people to send her their mixtapes: "I want your sad songs, your love jams, your sing-at-the-top-of-your-lungs car tunes, your break-up tape, your make-up tape, and your BFF-4evah cassette." The result: a charming collection of other people's mixtapes, from the universal "it's gonna be okay" mood-lifter to the perplexing yet intriguing "this is margerine on your toast" tape—which we are dying to listen to. On the right, another poster by Bingaman-Burt presents a selection from her "Daily Drawings" series that focuses on objects that help make things.

VANESSA'S

JENNI'S

MITCHELL'S

JENNIFER'S

ZACH'S

SHELLI'S

XEL'S

SPIKE

FRANK'S

ETHAN'S

PETRA'S

ANNA'S

ANGELA'S

JUDITH'S

DANIELLE'S

AMELIA'S

ELSIE'S

JENN'S

ZACH'S

MIKEY'S

CHARLOTTE'S

ALEX & VANESSA'S

JEN'S

OTHER PEOPLE'S PLANTS

ZACH & BRANDI'S

ADAM & ALLYN'S

## KATE BINGAMAN-BURT

*DAILY PURCHASE DRAWINGS: DRINKS & OTHER PEOPLE'S HOUSEPLANTS, 2008-2014/2014*

In her distinctive hand-drawn style, Kate Bingaman-Burt has here produced two screen prints. The first is a selection of drinks from her "Daily Purchase Drawings" project, and the second is an assortment of other people's plants. Both prints include delightful captions written by the artist that bring the drinks and plants to life, adding Bingaman-Burt's quirky touch that fans of the posters adore.

2727 NE GLISAN st.
PORTLAND, OR 97232
503.239.4444
dovevivipizza.com

PIZZA & DRINKS WITH BREANNE, NICOLE, SALLY & WILL

## RED VELVET
*from NAVARRE*

## EXTRACTO
AMERICANO PLUS SHORTBREAD COOKIE

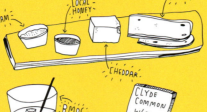

GRANOLA FRUIT & SOY MILK FROM CREMA

# SIZZLE PIE

## OLYMPIC PROVISIONS

DINNER W/ ZACH

BISCUITS & GRAVY + EGGS + COFFEE

## red and black
JAM    LOCAL HONEY    BREAD
CHEDDAR

BMOC
(BOURBON GINGER SODA & BITTERS)

CLYDE COMMON
W IAN (new mgmt)

DRAGON NOODLES
noodles, carrots, peanut sauce, nuts,

## SWEETPEA
BAKING Co.

## JASMINE RICE
+ MUU PING PORK SKEWERS
+ STEAMED VEGGIES
*from* PAADEE
6 SE 28TH AVE PDX

MAC
CHEESE
PORTLAND SOUP CO.

COOKIE
1.25
FROM FORD FOOD & DRINK

LOVELY'S
## Fifty Fifty
PIZZA, WINE & ICE CREAM
W/ VANESSA

## ScreenDoor    CANTEEN

½ CHICKEN & WAFFLES
½ BISCUITS & GRAVY
½ BACON PRALINE

PORTLAND BOWL (OMG)
quinoa / Black beans / Baked MAPLE TEMPEH /
NW SAUCE (anyone know what this is?) / KALE /
CARROTS / CHOPPED OREGON HAZELNUTS / YUM!

MARION BERRY GINGER SMOOTHIE
LAUGHING PLANET

## NONG'S KHAO MAN GAI

## Brunch
at SWEEDEEDEE

## Annies DONUTS
3449 NE 72ND AVE, PDX

## biwa
EXCELLENT DINNER with
ALLEN, JENNIFER, JEREMY & CLIFTON

## SPAGHETTI
FROM THE BYE & BYE

RICE
CHICKEN
SOYBEAN SAUCE
THE BEST
CUCUMBER

## DOUBLE DRAGON
PORTLAND BÁNH MÌ
Orange sesame soy curls ← favorite
BÁNH MÌ
THAI ICED TEA

## CHICKEN & WAFFLES
PLUS COFFEE PLUS ORANGE JUICE
PLUS THE JOY BRUNCH CLUB
from SIMPATICA.

## MORRISON HOTEL BAR
FRIES & BEER
BEFORE TYPHOON.
W/ZACH, BRANDI, IAN & STEVE.

## Miss DELTA
SOUTHERN STACK

## Waffles
+CHICKEN @SIMPATICA

# BO KE RA ME N
BOWL!
## CHICKEN PORK VEGGIES
FRIED CHICKEN ADD ON —
AWESOME.

## broder
Brunch → Breakfast Sandwich
• BAKED EGG
• CHEESE
• TOAST • HAM

## Croque Madame
BRUNCH! AT RADAR.

GRILLED CHEESE & TOMATO SOUP
from Ron Toms

## FALAFELS AND FRIES.
W/ ADAM @ ALEXANDRYA

## BREAK FAST FREAK ING BURRITO.
from Meat, Cheese, Bread.

## FORD FOOD + DRINK
THIS TRIP → orange cinnamon scone
& ICED COFFEE

## Kickstart
FROM CREMA

## APRISA
MEXICAN CUISINE
3 rancheno tacos

# yum YUM
PORTLAND, OR

PINK WEDGES

SNOWSHOES.

OXFORDS from RAD SUMMER

GREEN BOOTS

NEW FALL BOOTS

COWBOY BOOTS

Bass

LACEUP FLAT ESPADR

GRAY RAIN BOOTS.

AIR FLY STRONG

← TAN
← LEMON YELLOW

COLE HAAN

foldable flats.

JEFFREY CAMPBELL PREP TASSELED LOAFER

Blue Suede

Orange Sole.

WÖRISHOFER 562

WHITE LEATHER OXFORDS

MINNETONKA MOCCASIN

SUMMER SHOES

HOT PINK

Clarks® BRONZE OXFORDS

MINNETONKA boatmoc ---> BRIGHT YELLOW

LET'S STOP BUYING SHOES.

BROWN BOOTS

DR. MARTENS 7-EYE BOOT

REPLACEMENT SANDALS

BASS OXFORD COLOR: NICKEL

SLIPPERS

SHOES SHOES SHOES

## KATE BINGAMAN-BURT
*DAILY PURCHASE DRAWINGS: PORTLAND FOOD & DAILY PURCHASE DRAWINGS SHOES, 2009-2014/2006-2014*

Red velvet cake, sizzle pie, jasmine rice, a croque madame, and falafel. A perfect example of globalization's impact on the availability of different kinds of foods in any given city, this print by Kate Bingaman-Burt displays the wide variety of meals you can expect to eat when in Portland, Oregon. On the right, a selection of shoes from the designer's "Daily Purchase Drawings" series hand-drawn in a sweet palette of grays, blues, and pinks.

# HARUKI MURAKAMI
# BINGO

GRANT SNIDER
*HARUKI MURAKAMI BINGO & DAY JOBS OF THE POETS, 2012/2013*

The novels of Haruki Murakami are full of recurring surreal characters and themes. After reading nearly all of his books, Grant Snider created this bingo card to play while rereading the novels. The illustration was published in the **New York Times**'s Book Review. On the right, Snider compiled a few notable poets and created a rhyming ensemble of their day jobs (some real, others fictional) to be read from left to right. As an orthodontist by day, Snider was fascinated by artists who had a career far removed from their creative life.

# DAY JOBS OF THE POETS

WILLIAM CARLOS WILLIAMS, PEDIATRICIAN
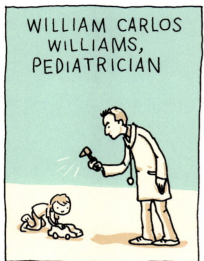

W.B. YEATS, OCCULT MAGICIAN

WALLACE STEVENS, INSURANCE SALESMAN

CHARLES BUKOWSKI, DISGRUNTLED MAILMAN

MAYA ANGELOU, NIGHTCLUB CROONER

HERMAN MELVILLE, ASPIRING HARPOONER

PHILIP LARKIN, PUBLIC LIBRARIAN

ROBERT FROST, FAILED AGRARIAN
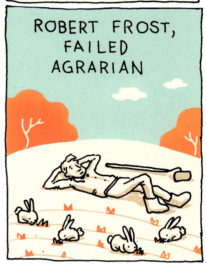

T. S. ELIOT, BANK CLERK

JACK KEROUAC, RAILROAD WORK

PABLO NERUDA, DIPLOMAT

EMILY DICKINSON, KEEPER OF CATS

VINEGAR
(MOSTLY AS AN APPETITE SUPPRESANT. HE HAD EATING ISSUES.)

LORD BYRON

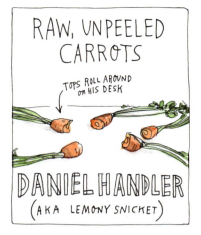

RAW, UNPEELED CARROTS

TOPS ROLL AROUND ON HIS DESK

DANIEL HANDLER
(AKA LEMONY SNICKET)

ESPRESSO, ESPRESSO, ESPRESSO

MARCEL PROUST

TEA OUT of A GLASS

PU'ER TEA

ROASTED ALMONDS for BREAKS

MICHAEL POLLAN

OYSTERS + MEAT
(for BREAKFAST!)

WALT WHITMAN

PRETTY-NEAR-RAW BEEF PHO

and CORN NUTS!

MARY ROACH

COLD TOAST and STALE COFFEE

COFFEE RINGS

JOHN STEINBECK

HER OWN HOME-BAKED BREAD

PRIZE WINNING INDIAN and RYE

EMILY DICKINSON

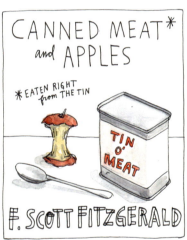

CANNED MEAT* and APPLES

* EATEN RIGHT from THE TIN

TIN O' MEAT

F. SCOTT FITZGERALD

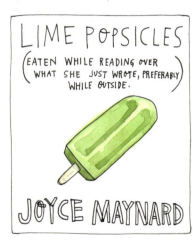

LIME POPSICLES
(EATEN WHILE READING OVER WHAT SHE JUST WROTE, PREFERABLY WHILE OUTSIDE.)

JOYCE MAYNARD

COFFEE
11 A.M.

MINT TEA
12 P.M.

SHERRY
2 P.M.

MARTINI
4 P.M.

TRUMAN CAPOTE

MILK

FRANZ KAFKA

**WENDY MACNAUGHTON**
*SNACKS OF THE GREAT SCRIBBLERS, 2011*

Writer and illustrator Wendy MacNaughton wondered what fuel writers have relied on in order to keep their creativity flowing, and the answers are as diverse as the writers' styles, as can be seen in this light-hearted infographic.

**GRANT SNIDER**
*SKETCHBOOKS OF THE PROS, 2012*

A sketchbook can provide a lot of insight into its owner's personality. Humorously imagining the sketchbooks of people in various disciplines, Grant Snider envisions abstract expressionists to be as gifted as elephants, and perfectionists to be the most boring sketchers of all.

# SKETCHBOOKS OF THE PROS

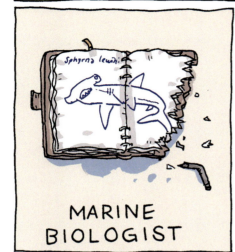

MARINE
BIOLOGIST

COMMUTER

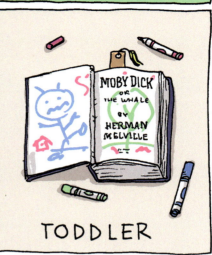

TODDLER

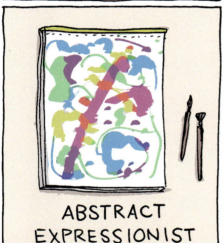

ABSTRACT
EXPRESSIONIST

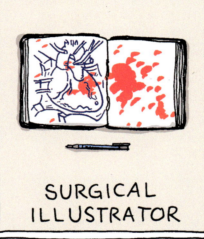

SURGICAL
ILLUSTRATOR

ANTHROPOMORPHIST
ARCHITECT

ELEPHANT

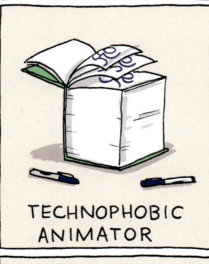

TECHNOPHOBIC
ANIMATOR

SELF-CENSORING
PORTRAITIST

FRUSTRATED
ORIGAMIST

ILLITERATE
TYPOGRAPHER

PERFECTIONIST

HEADS DOWN

# BINGO CALLS

HOUSE!

| Number One | Number Two | Number Three | Number Four | Number Five | Number Six | Number Seven | Number Eight | Number Nine | Number Ten |
|---|---|---|---|---|---|---|---|---|---|
| Kelly's Eye | One Little Duck | Cup of Tea | Knock at the Door | Man Alive! | Tom Mix | Lucky Seven | Garden Gate | Doctor's Orders | PM's Den |
| Legs Eleven | Number Twelve | Unlucky For Some | Valentine's Day | Number Fifteen | Sweet Sixteen | Seventeen | Coming of Age | Goodbye Teens | Number Twenty |
| Number Eleven | Monkey's Cousin | Number Thirteen | Number Fourteen | Young & Keen | Never Been Kissed | Dancing Queen | Number Eighteen | Number Nineteen | Getting Plenty |
| Key of the Door | Two Little Ducks | The Lord is My Shepherd | Twenty-Four | Twenty-Five | Bed & Breakfast | Duck & A Crutch | Twenty-Eight | Twenty-Nine | Dirty Gertie |
| Twenty-One | Twenty-Two | Twenty-Three | Do You Want Some More? | Duck & Dive | Twenty-Six | Twenty-Seven | Overweight | Rise & Shine | Number Thirty |
| Thirty-One | Thirty-Two | Thirty-Three | Thirty-Four | Thirty-Five | Perfect Figure | Thirty-Seven | Thirty-Eight | Those Famous Steps | Naughty Forty |
| Get Up & Run | Buckle My Shoe | Dirty Knees | Ask For More | Jump & Jive | Thirty-Six | A Flea in Heaven | Christmas Cake | Thirty-Nine | Number Forty |
| Forty-One | Forty-Two | Forty-Three | Forty-Four | Halfway House | Forty-Six | Four & Seven | Four Dozen | Police Constable | Bull's Eye |
| Time For Fun | Winnie the Pooh | Down on Your Knees | Droopy Drawers | Forty-Five | Up To Tricks | Forty-Seven | Forty-Eight | Forty-Nine | Number Fifty |
| Fifty-One | Fifty-Two | Fifty-Three | The House of Bamboo | Snakes Alive! | Fifty-Six | Heinz Beans | Fifty-Eight | Fifty-Nine | Blind Sixty |
| I Love My Mum | Danny La Rue | Stuck in a Tree | Number Fifty-Four | Fifty-Five | Was She Worth It? | Fifty-Seven | Make 'Em Wait | Brighton Line | Number Sixty |
| Sixty-One | Sixty-Two | Sixty-Three | That Beatles Number | Stop Work | Sixty-Six | Sixty-Seven | Sixty-Eight | Dinner for Two | Three Score & Ten |
| Baker's Bun | Tickety-Boo | Tickle Me | Sixty-Four | Sixty-Five | Clickety Click | Made in Heaven | Saving Grace | Sixty-Nine | Number Seventy |
| Seventy-One | Par for the Course | Seventy-Three | Seventy-Four | Seventy-Five | Seventy-Six | Seventy-Seven | Seventy-Eight | Seventy-Nine | Gandhi's Breakfast |
| Bang on the Drum | Seventy-Two | Queen Bee | Candy Store | Strive & Strive | Trombones | Sunset Strip | Heaven's Gate | One More Time | Number Eighty |
| Eighty-One | Eighty-Two | Eighty-Three | Seven Dozen | Eighty-Five | Eighty-Six | Eighty-Seven | Two Fat Ladies | Nearly There | Top of the Shop |
| Stop & Run | Straight on Through | Time for Tea | Eighty-Four | Staying Alive | Between the Sticks | Torquay in Devon | Eighty-Eight | Eighty-Nine | Number Ninety |

# THE COCKNEY ALPHABET

**A** for 'ORSES
**B** for MUTTON
**C** for MILES
**D** for DUMB
**E** for BRICK
**F** for LUMP
**G** for POLICE
**H** for RETIREMENT
**I** for NOVELLO
**J** for ORANGES
**K** for RESTAURANT
**L** for LEATHER
**M** for SIS
**N** for EGGS
**O** for THE FENCE
**P** for RELIEF
**Q** for A BUS
**R** for COCK LINNET*
**S** for YOU
**T** for GUMS
**U** for ME
**V** for LA FRANCE
**W** for A QUID
**X** for BREAKFAST
**Y** for MISTRESS
**Z** for BREEZE

PEARLY KING
PIE & MASH
COSTERMONGER
PEARLY QUEEN

*rhyming slang: a minute     a Troynovant Peculiar

**PAUL BOMMER**
*BINGO CALLS & THE COCKNEY ALPHABET
2013/2013*

These two witty screen prints by Paul Bommer, an illustrator and graphic designer based in London's East End, pair images and words with a lot of humor, inviting the viewer to take a closer look.

# EUROPEAN CITIES } ABC

- AMSTERDAM -
- BARCELONA -
- COPENHAGEN -
- DUBLIN -
- EDINBURGH -
- FRANKFURT -
- GENEVA -
- HELSINKI -
- ISTANBUL -
- JEREZ DE LA FRONTERA -
- KIEV -
- LONDON -
- MADRID -
- NAPLES -
- OSLO -
- PARIS -
- QUIMPER -
- ROME -
- STOCKHOLM -
- TOULOUSE -
- UTRECHT -
- VENISE -
- WARSAW -
- XANTEN -
- YORK -
- ZAGREB -

## HUGO YOSHIKAWA
*EUROPEAN CITIES ABC, 2012*

From Amsterdam to Zagreb, French-Japanese illustrator Hugo Yoshikawa chose 26 European cities to represent the alphabet. He researched and used their most notable sights and symbols to form the shape of each city's first letter.

# A PARTIAL INVENTORY OF
# GUSTAVE FLAUBERT'S PERSONAL EFFECTS

As Catalogued by M. Lemoel on MAY 20, 1880, Twelve Days after the Writer's Death.

In the bedroom on the first floor, panama hat, top hat, red silk cravat, 5 pairs of gloves, 49 shirts, 2 dressing gowns, 5 waistcoats, 7 walking sticks, tobacco jar, two pairs of boots. In the dining room, 35 champagne glasses, 48 porcelain dinner plates, a painting representing Napoleon I, a pocket watch in a gold case engraved with initials 'G.F.,' a gold watch chain, a gold signet ring with square stone, a silver spoon and two forks marked 'N Flaubert,' 5 oyster-knives with black handles and silver blades. In the study on the first floor, engraving in oakwood frame representing THE TEMPTATION OF SAINT ANTOINE by Callot, marble clock with bronze figurines, maker's name 'Dortigny' engraved on dial, photographic reproduction of painting entitled VISIONS, array consisting of lances, javelins, arrows, mandolin, Basque drum, axe, oriental pipe, cardboard Chinese statuette, large round table in mahogany, green woolen tablecloth, one tiger skin, one lynx skin, one bear skin, white, penholder in the shape of a dragon, bronze inkwell, three paperknives, one with initials 'G.F.,' two Egyptian lanterns, unfinished manuscript entitled BOUVARD ET PÉCUCHET, Creuzer, RELIGIONS OF ANTIQUITY in 11 vols., works of Saint Theresa in Migne edition, works of Walter Scott in 32 vols. In the drawer of one of the small bookcases is found the sum of 2545 francs, which sum is deposited with Maître Bidault to cover funeral expenses, burial charges, and other debts.

## JOANNA NEBORSKY
*A PARTIAL INVENTORY OF GUSTAVE FLAU-BERT'S PERSONAL EFFECTS, JULY 2012*

The New York-based illustrator Joanna Neborsky is a book lover. When she picked up Geoffrey Wall's **Flaubert: A Life,** she found the list of Flaubert's belongings in the back of the biography. This poster catalogues 155 objects found in Gustave Flaubert's house on May 20th 1880, twelve days after the writer's death. With poetic succinctness, the deceptively simple drawings show a selection of his personal effects, including 35 champagne glasses, 48 porcelain dinner plates, a gold watch chain, and a penholder in the shape of a dragon.

# UNTRANSLATABLE WORDS

1. AGE-TORI (JAPANESE): TO LOOK WORSE AFTER A HAIRCUT. 2. BACKPFEIFENGESICHT (GERMAN): A FACE IN NEED OF A SLAP. 3. CRAIC (IRISH): FUN, AMUSEMENT, ENTERTAINING COMPANY OR CONVERSATION. 4. DOZYWOCIE (POLISH): PARENTAL CONTRACT WITH CHILDREN GUARANTEEING LIFELONG SUPPORT. 5. EIDOLON (ANCIENT GREEK): PHANTOM LOOK-ALIKE TAKING THE FORM OF A LIVING OR DEAD PERSON. 6. FIKA (SWEDISH): RELAXED SOCIAL EVENT WITH GOOD FRIENDS INVOLVING COFFEE AND PASTRIES. 7. GIGIL (FILIPINO): THE IRRESISTIBLE URGE TO PINCH OR SQUEEZE SOMETHING CUTE. 8. HANYAUKU (KWANGALI): THE ART OF WALKING ON TIPTOES ACROSS WARM SAND. 9. ISTORIES ME ARKOUDES (GREEK): LITERALLY 'STORIES WITH BEARS', NARRATED EVENTS WHICH ARE TOO FAR FETCHED TO BE TRUE. 10. JANTELOVEN (DANISH & NORWEGIAN): THE LAW OF JANTE, RULES WHICH DISCOURAGE INDIVIDUAL THOUGHT WITHIN COMMUNITIES. 11. KOMOREBI (JAPANESE): DAPPLED SUNLIGHT THROUGH TREES. 12. L'APPEL DU VIDE (FRENCH): LITERALLY 'THE CALL OF THE VOID', THE URGE TO JUMP FROM A HEIGHT. 13. MAMIHLAPINATAPAI (YAGHAN): A SHARED LOOK OF DESIRE WHICH NEITHER PARTY ARE WILLING TO INITIATE ACTION UPON. 14. NEIDBAU (GERMAN): A BUILDING CONSTRUCTED WITH THE SOLE PURPOSE OF INCONVENIENCING A NEIGHBOUR. 15. OPPHOLDSVEIR (NORWEGIAN): WEATHER JUST AFTER THE RAIN HAS STOPPED. 16. POSHLOST (RUSSIAN): SELF-SATISFIED VULGARITY MASQUERADING AS HIGH MORALITY. 17. QUALUNQUISMO (ITALIAN): APATHY AND INDIFFERENCE TOWARDS POLITICS. 18. RENAO (MANDARIN): LIVELY, FESTIVE, HAPPY AND NOISY. 19. SNORKER (EARLY ENGLISH): ONE WHO PRIES INTO OTHERS' BUSINESS. 20. TARTLE (SCOTTISH): THE ACT OF HESITATION WHEN INTRODUCING SOMEONE AFTER FORGETTING THEIR NAME. 21. UITWAAIEN (DUTCH): LITERALLY 'TO WALK IN THE WIND', TO TAKE A BRIEF BREAK OUTSIDE TO CLEAR ONE'S HEAD. 22. VOMITORIUM (LATIN): ERROR - A ROOM FOR VOMITING, POPULARIZED BY ALDOUS HUXLEY, ACTUALLY A PASSAGEWAY IN A THEATRE. 23. WALDEINSAMKEIT (GERMAN): FEELING OF BEING PEACEFULLY ALONE IN THE WOODS. 24. XINKU (MANDARIN): THANKING SOMEONE WHILE ACKNOWLEDGING THEIR HARD WORK. 25. YUANFEN (MANDARIN): BINDING FORCE WHICH EVENTUALLY BRINGS TWO PEOPLE TOGETHER IN LOVE. 26. ZHAGHZHAGH (PERSIAN): CHATTERING OF TEETH FROM COLD OR RAGE.

**FUCHSIA MACAREE**
*A-Z OF UNTRANSLATABLE WORDS, 2012*

Fuchsia Macaree is interested in language, a subject that she tackled beautifully in this engaging alphabet of words that cannot be translated into English. Looking at each word's origin, one can catch a glimpse into the country's culture, such as the Kwangali word "hanyauku," meaning "the act of walking on tiptoes across warm sand," which enables us to imagine Namibian landscapes.

**POST TYPOGRAPHY**
*KNOWLEDGE THAT WORKS, 2011*

For their "Knowledge That Works" campaign, the University of Baltimore asked Post Typography to come up with an engaging way of showcasing the range of academic pursuits available at the institution. Each letter of this illustration represents a different type of chart, graph, or other visual representation of information.

COOKING MEALS

WASHING DISHES

BUYING GROCERIES

WASHING AND IRONING CLOTHES

DOING MANUAL WORK

TAKING CARE OF PLANTS AND PETS

GIVING FOOD TO THE CHILDREN

PLAYING WITH KIDS

TRANSPORTING THE KIDS

CLEANING

ADMIN TASKS

**FRANCESCO MUZZI**
*WHO IS WORKING AT HOME? &
PRODUCTIVE ARCHETYPES 2014/2013*

A thought-provoking illustration of 11 tasks shared by married couples every week in Switzerland, "Who Is Working At Home?" might or might not surprise you. The gender represented for each job reflects the person who, on average, spends the most amount of time on that particular task. "Productive Archetypes," on the other hand, lightheartedly shows the various behaviors one can have towards work, from the juggling "multitasker" to the overzealous "connector."

THE MULTITASKER

THE MONOTASKER

THE LONE
WOLF

THE FIREFIGHTER

THE PROCRASTINATOR

THE EARLY BIRD

THE NIGHT OWL

THE CONNECTOR

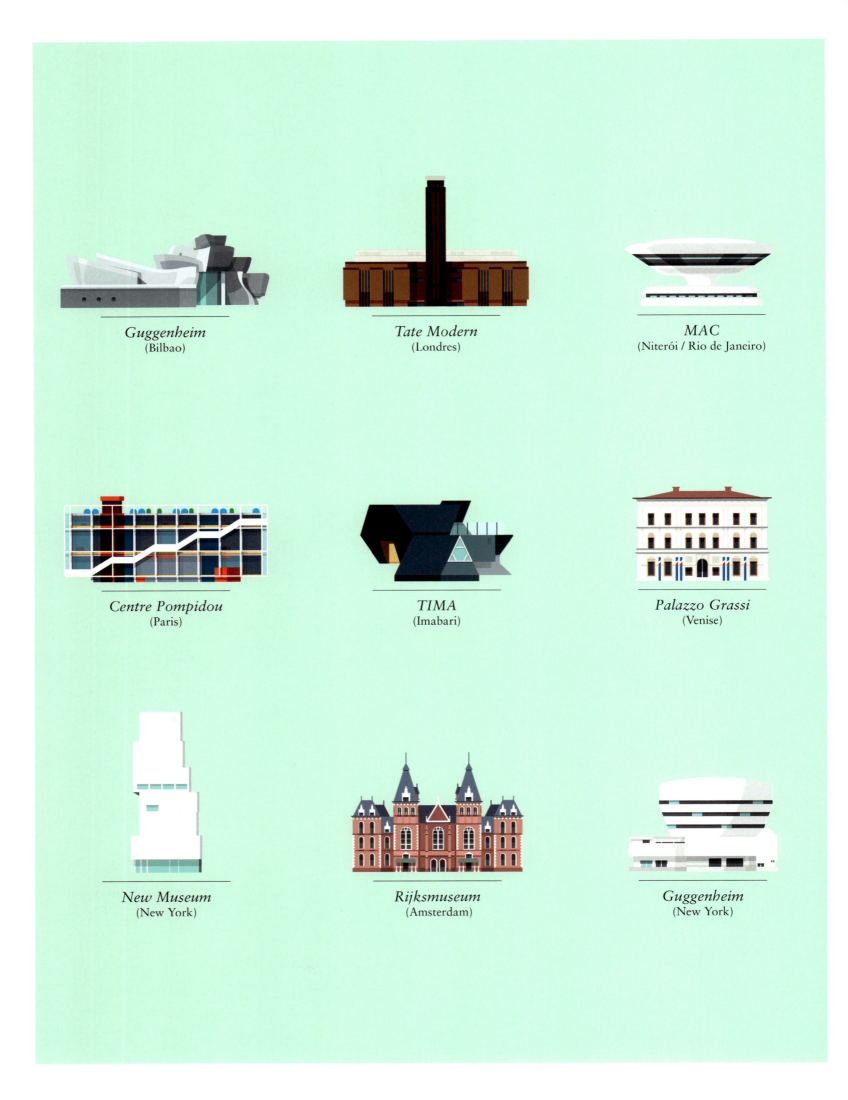

Guggenheim
(Bilbao)

Tate Modern
(Londres)

MAC
(Niterói / Rio de Janeiro)

Centre Pompidou
(Paris)

TIMA
(Imabari)

Palazzo Grassi
(Venise)

New Museum
(New York)

Rijksmuseum
(Amsterdam)

Guggenheim
(New York)

**LE DUO**
LE DUO FOR IDEAT MAGAZINE, 2014

These two images by Parisian design studio Le Duo were commissioned by **Ideat Magazine** to illustrate the "Contemporary Trips" and "Contemporary Lifestyle" sections of their April 2014 issue. Known for their clear, innovative visuals, Le Duo were a perfect match for the French home-décor magazine.

*Famille «Hipsters»*
(New York)

*Famille «Arty»*
(Berlin)

*Famille «Healthy»*
(Los Angeles)

*Famille «Urban chic»*
(Londres)

*Famille «Afro»*
(Dakar)

*Famille «Bobo»*
(Paris)

*Famille «Business»*
(Shanghai)

*Famille «Hippie chic»*
(Amsterdam)

*Famille «Fashion»*
(Milan)

ROBIN DAVEY
HOW TO GET A JOB 2013

The **Times** commissioned "How To Get A Job" for the cover of a pullout section aimed at recent graduates. Straightforward both graphically and conceptually, the illustration consists of a grid of characters dressed for a variety of careers. Robin Davey explains that "they are intended as types rather than individuals."

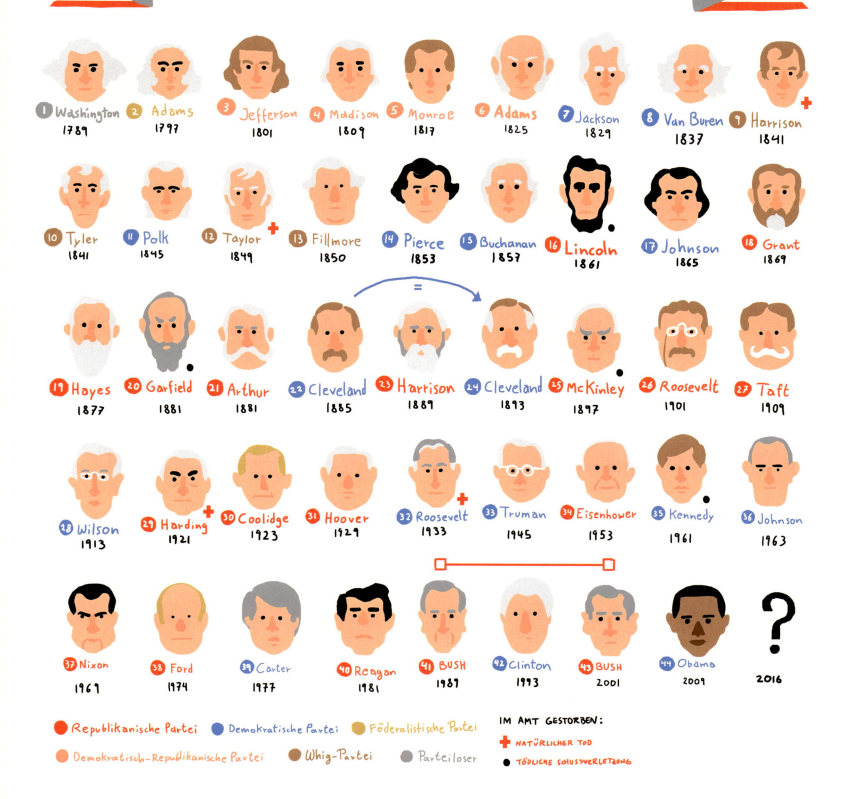

# PRÄSIDENTEN DER USA

| | | | | | | | | |
|---|---|---|---|---|---|---|---|---|
| 1 Washington 1789 | 2 Adams 1797 | 3 Jefferson 1801 | 4 Madison 1809 | 5 Monroe 1817 | 6 Adams 1825 | 7 Jackson 1829 | 8 Van Buren 1837 | 9 Harrison 1841 |
| 10 Tyler 1841 | 11 Polk 1845 | 12 Taylor 1849 | 13 Fillmore 1850 | 14 Pierce 1853 | 15 Buchanan 1857 | 16 Lincoln 1861 | 17 Johnson 1865 | 18 Grant 1869 |
| 19 Hayes 1877 | 20 Garfield 1881 | 21 Arthur 1881 | 22 Cleveland 1885 | 23 Harrison 1889 | 24 Cleveland 1893 | 25 McKinley 1897 | 26 Roosevelt 1901 | 27 Taft 1909 |
| 28 Wilson 1913 | 29 Harding 1921 | 30 Coolidge 1923 | 31 Hoover 1929 | 32 Roosevelt 1933 | 33 Truman 1945 | 34 Eisenhower 1953 | 35 Kennedy 1961 | 36 Johnson 1963 |
| 37 Nixon 1969 | 38 Ford 1974 | 39 Carter 1977 | 40 Reagan 1981 | 41 BUSH 1989 | 42 Clinton 1993 | 43 BUSH 2001 | 44 Obama 2009 | ? 2016 |

● Republikanische Partei   ● Demokratische Partei   ● Föderalistische Partei

● Demokratisch-Republikanische Partei   ● Whig-Partei   ● Parteiloser

IM AMT GESTORBEN:

✚ NATÜRLICHER TOD

● TÖDLICHE SCHUSSVERLETZUNG

MATTHIAS SCHÜTTE
*PRÄSIDENTEN DER USA, 2012*

Inspired by the 2012 presidential elections in the United States, German illustrator Matthias Schütte created this informative graphic of all the U.S. presidents. The 2012 elections now having passed, Schütte changed the year underneath the question mark to "2016." A question that many people would like to know the answer to!

# BUILDINGS OF NEW YORK CITY

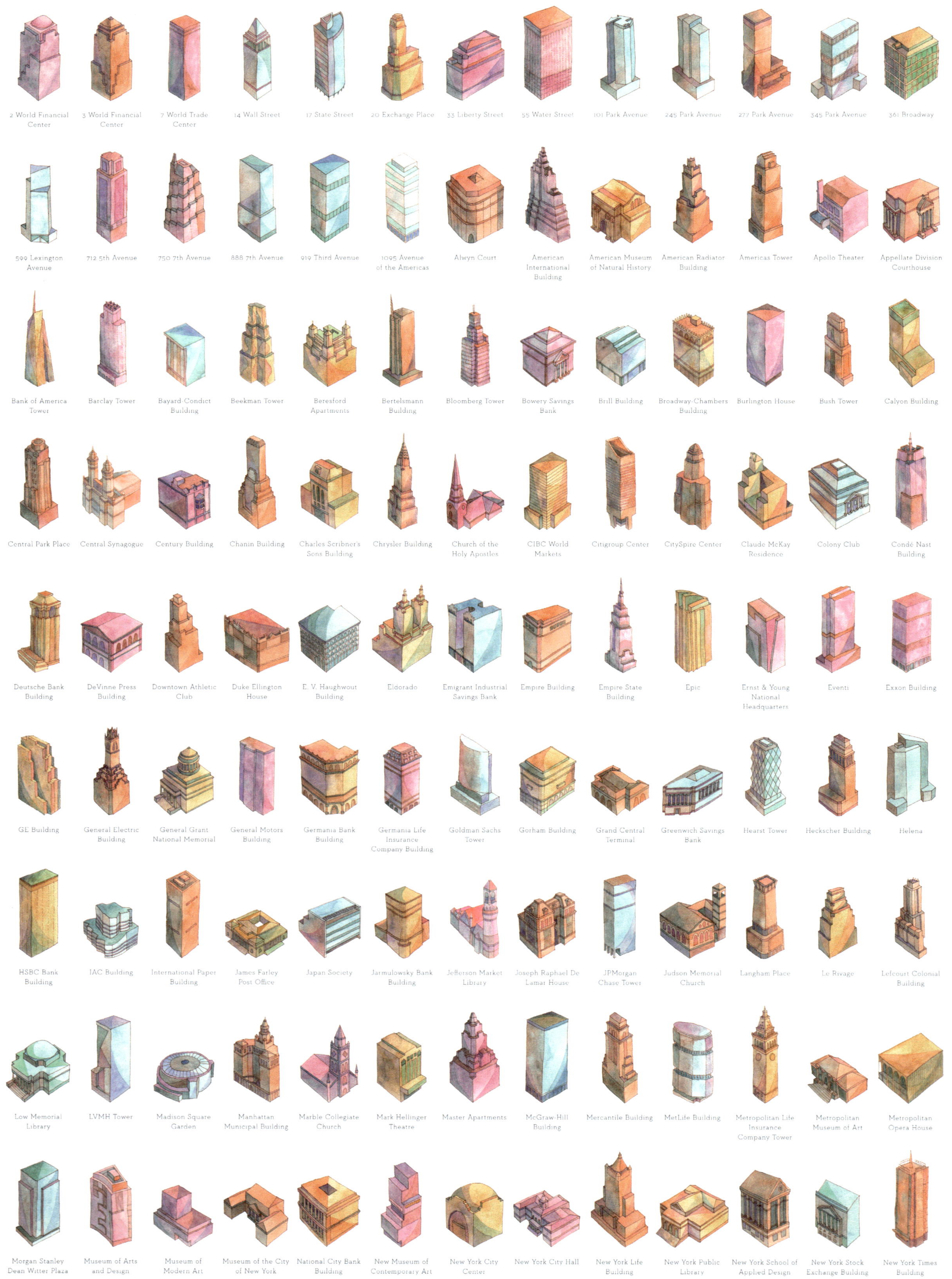
2 World Financial Center
3 World Financial Center
7 World Trade Center
14 Wall Street
17 State Street
20 Exchange Place
33 Liberty Street
55 Water Street
101 Park Avenue
245 Park Avenue
277 Park Avenue
345 Park Avenue
361 Broadway
599 Lexington Avenue
712 5th Avenue
750 7th Avenue
888 7th Avenue
919 Third Avenue
1095 Avenue of the Americas
Alwyn Court
American International Building
American Museum of Natural History
American Radiator Building
Americas Tower
Apollo Theater
Appellate Division Courthouse
Bank of America Tower
Barclay Tower
Bayard-Condict Building
Beekman Tower
Beresford Apartments
Bertelsmann Building
Bloomberg Tower
Bowery Savings Bank
Brill Building
Broadway-Chambers Building
Burlington House
Bush Tower
Calyon Building
Central Park Place
Central Synagogue
Century Building
Chanin Building
Charles Scribner's Sons Building
Chrysler Building
Church of the Holy Apostles
CIBC World Markets
Citigroup Center
CitySpire Center
Claude McKay Residence
Colony Club
Condé Nast Building
Deutsche Bank Building
DeVinne Press Building
Downtown Athletic Club
Duke Ellington House
E. V. Haughwout Building
Eldorado
Emigrant Industrial Savings Bank
Empire Building
Empire State Building
Epic
Ernst & Young National Headquarters
Eventi
Exxon Building
GE Building
General Electric Building
General Grant National Memorial
General Motors Building
Germania Bank Building
Germania Life Insurance Company Building
Goldman Sachs Tower
Gorham Building
Grand Central Terminal
Greenwich Savings Bank
Hearst Tower
Heckscher Building
Helena
HSBC Bank Building
IAC Building
International Paper Building
James Farley Post Office
Japan Society
Jarmulowsky Bank Building
Jefferson Market Library
Joseph Raphael De Lamar House
JPMorgan Chase Tower
Judson Memorial Church
Langham Place
Le Rivage
Lefcourt Colonial Building
Low Memorial Library
LVMH Tower
Madison Square Garden
Manhattan Municipal Building
Marble Collegiate Church
Mark Hellinger Theatre
Master Apartments
McGraw-Hill Building
Mercantile Building
MetLife Building
Metropolitan Life Insurance Company Tower
Metropolitan Museum of Art
Metropolitan Opera House
Morgan Stanley Dean Witter Plaza
Museum of Arts and Design
Museum of Modern Art
Museum of the City of New York
National City Bank Building
New Museum of Contemporary Art
New York City Center
New York City Hall
New York Life Building
New York Public Library
New York School of Applied Design
New York Stock Exchange Building
New York Times Building

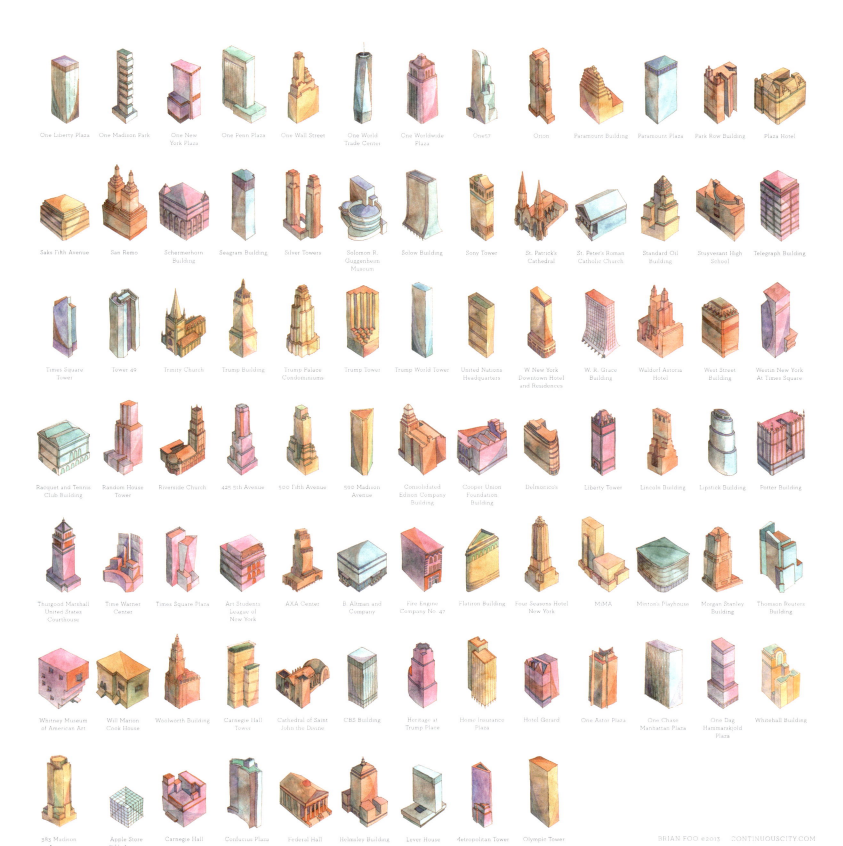

One Liberty Plaza | One Madison Park | One New York Plaza | One Penn Plaza | One Wall Street | One World Trade Center | One Worldwide Plaza | One57 | Orion | Paramount Building | Paramount Plaza | Park Row Building | Plaza Hotel

Saks Fifth Avenue | San Remo | Schermerhorn Building | Seagram Building | Silver Towers | Solomon R. Guggenheim Museum | Solow Building | Sony Tower | St. Patrick's Cathedral | St. Peter's Roman Catholic Church | Standard Oil Building | Stuyvesant High School | Telegraph Building

Times Square Tower | Tower 49 | Trinity Church | Trump Building | Trump Palace Condominiums | Trump Tower | Trump World Tower | United Nations Headquarters | W New York Downtown Hotel and Residences | W. R. Grace Building | Waldorf Astoria Hotel | West Street Building | Westin New York At Times Square

Racquet and Tennis Club Building | Random House Tower | Riverside Church | 425 5th Avenue | 500 Fifth Avenue | 590 Madison Avenue | Consolidated Edison Company Building | Cooper Union Foundation Building | Delmonico's | Liberty Tower | Lincoln Building | Lipstick Building | Potter Building

Thurgood Marshall United States Courthouse | Time Warner Center | Times Square Plaza | Art Students League of New York | AXA Center | B. Altman and Company | Fire Engine Company No. 47 | Flatiron Building | Four Seasons Hotel New York | MiMA | Minton's Playhouse | Morgan Stanley Building | Thomson Reuters Building

Whitney Museum of American Art | Will Marion Cook House | Woolworth Building | Carnegie Hall Tower | Cathedral of Saint John the Divine | CBS Building | Heritage at Trump Place | Home Insurance Plaza | Hotel Gerard | One Astor Plaza | One Chase Manhattan Plaza | One Dag Hammarskjold Plaza | Whitehall Building

383 Madison Avenue | Apple Store Fifth Avenue | Carnegie Hall | Confucius Plaza | Federal Hall | Helmsley Building | Lever House | Metropolitan Tower | Olympic Tower

BRIAN FOO ©2013   CONTINUOUSCITY.COM

## BRIAN FOO
*CONTINUOUS CITY, 2013*

Brian Foo is a designer and web developer who writes about art and coding, and who thinks that "art should be more accessible, personal, and impactful." For his ongoing project "Continuous Cities," Foo has painted hundreds of New York City buildings using ink and watercolors, and raised over $19,000 on Kickstarter in order to turn the drawings into a book that explores imagined landscapes and topographies for the city and builds an interactive platform online where people will be able to create, narrate, and share their own versions of the Big Apple.

Statue of Liberty    NY Life Building    Chrysler Building    20 Exchange Plaza    70 Pine Street (American International Building)    UN Headquarters    One Chase Manhattan Plaza    One Penn Plaza    One Astor Plaza
        Woolworth Building    The Trump Building    Empire State Building    GE Building    JP Morgan Chase World Headquarters    MetLife Building    Seagram Veteran Building    One Astor Plaza    One Liberty Plaza

COLOS

SEOUL    CHICAGO

## YONI ALTER

*COLOSSAL NYC PRINT & SHAPES OF CITIES PRINTS, 2013/2013-ONGOING*

All major cities have their own iconic buildings that are distinguishable by their shape.
Chicago has its Trump Tower, Berlin is mostly
known for the Fernsehturm, and New York
City has quite a few colossal constructions
that define its cityscape, such as the Chrysler
and the Empire State Buildings. "Colossal NYC
Print" includes chronologically ordered structures, as well as buildings that were expected
to be completed in 2013. For his illustrations,
London-based designer Yoni Alter uses only
stylized silhouettes yet achieves a highly recognizable depiction of each skyline.

| | | | | | | |
|---|---|---|---|---|---|---|
| | | **01**<br>**Ih** | | | | |
| | | **02**<br>**Wh** | **03**<br>**In** | | | |
| | | **05**<br>**Hh** | **04**<br>**Ft** | | | |
| | | **06**<br>**Mv** | **07**<br>**Ch** | | | |
| | | **08**<br>**Mh** | **09**<br>**Mg** | **10**<br>**Eh** | | |
| | | **12**<br>**Mv** | **13**<br>**Cp** | **11**<br>**Ri** | | |
| | | **14**<br>**Uw** | **16**<br>**Ca** | **17**<br>**Wi** | | |
| | **15**<br>**Ls** | **18**<br>**Sp** | **19**<br>**Ue** | **20**<br>**Yv** | | |
| | **22**<br>**Cl** | **23**<br>**M** | **24**<br>**Ts** | **21**<br>**Lh** | **27**<br>**Rv** | |
| | **25**<br>**Ce** | **26**<br>**Ms** | **28**<br>**Mu** | **29**<br>**Kb** | **30**<br>**Mc** | |
| | **33**<br>**Wv** | **34**<br>**Fi** | **31**<br>**Gr** | **32**<br>**St** | | |
| | **35**<br>**Gv** | **36**<br>**So** | **38**<br>**No** | **39**<br>**Ev** | | |
| | **42**<br>**Tr** | **37**<br>**Li** | **40**<br>**Ct** | **41**<br>**Le** | | |
| | **43**<br>**Bp** | **44**<br>**C** | | | | |
| | **45**<br>**Fd** | | | | | |

**PERIODIC TABLE MANHATTAN**

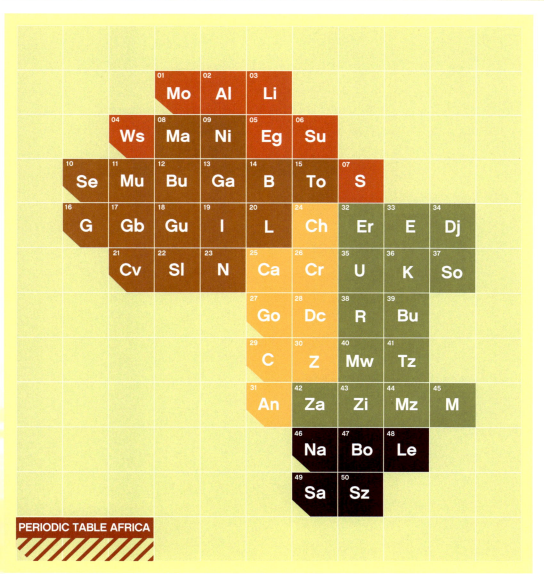

### VIGILISM

*PERIODIC MAPS, 2011*

What looks like chemistry is actually another way of mapping our world. Created in the style of the periodic table of elements, this colorful series depicts Africa, the United States, and Manhattan in a new light. By using some of his favorite places as subjects, Brooklyn-based Lekan Jeyifous explores new methods of communicating information in a visually stimulating way.

**1992-93**
Olympiastadion, Munich

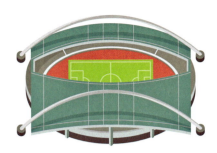

**1993-94**
Olympic Stadium, Athens

**1994-95**
Ernst-Happel-Stadion, Vienna

**1995-96**
Stadio Olimpico, Rome

**1996-97**
Olympiastadion, Munich

**1997-98**
Amsterdam Arena, Amsterdam

**1998-99**
Camp Nou, Barcelona

**1999-2000**
Stade de France, Saint-Denis

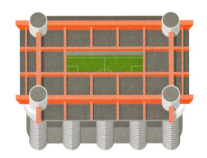

**2000-01**
San Siro, Milan

**JACOPO FERRETTI**
*UEFA CHAMPIONS LEAGUE STADIUMS*
*1993-2013, 2013*

In chronological order spanning ten years' time starting in 1993, this visual collection groups 17 famous stadiums that hosted the UEFA Champions League Finals. Clean lines and vibrant colors show each venue's distinctive traits and concisely highlight the stadiums' different features.

**2001-02**
Hampden Park, Glasgow

**2002-03**
Old Trafford, Manchester

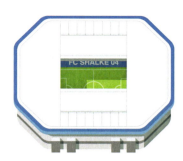

**2003-04**
Arena AufSchalke, Gelsenkirchen

**2004-05**
Atatürk Olympic Stadium, Istanbul

**2005-06**
Stade de France, Saint-Denis

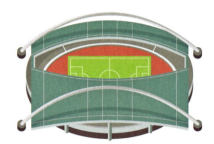

**2006-07**
Olympic Stadium, Athens

**2007-08**
Luzhniki Stadium, Moscow

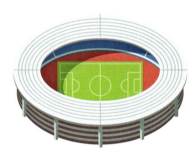

**2008-09**
Stadio Olimpico, Rome

**2009-10**
antiago Bernabéu Stadium, Madrid

**2010-11**
Wembley Stadium, London

**2011-12**
Allianz Arena, Munich

**2012-13**
Wembley Stadium, London

**ADAM SIMPSON**
*TENTS &*
*PERSONALISED MEDICINE, 2011*

In an era when people seek to reconnect with nature as a way of momentarily fleeing over-stimulated urban lives, camping has never been more in style. From the minimal tipi to the fully equipped dome, tents are at the core of any successful camping trip. In this print, Adam Simpson celebrates their simple charm. The next witty work matches a group of people with their corresponding pills. A visually compelling commentary on the way medication has become the easy-fix answer to all our woes. "Personalised Medicine" makes a strong statement using a deceivingly cheerful aesthetic with vivid colors and silhouetted lines.

## UN BICCHIERE DI ESTATHÈ

22 grammi

## UNA CAROTA

1 grammo

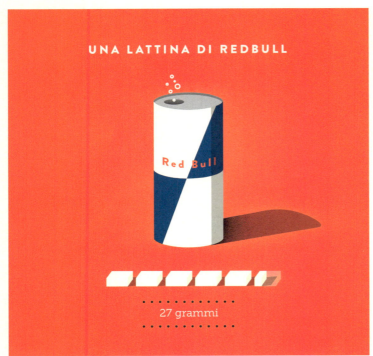

## UNA LATTINA DI REDBULL

27 grammi

## UNPACCHETTO DI OREO

15 grammi

## UNA LATTINA DI COCA-COLA

39 grammi

## UN BICCHIERE MEDIO DI MILKSHAKE AL CIOCCOLATO

111 grammi

UN BICCHIERE
DI LATTE DI SOIA

7 grammi

UN HAMBURGER SEMPLICE
McDONALD'S

8,5 grammi

UNA PORZIONE DI
KETCHUP

5 grammi

UNA PALLINA DI GELATO
HÄAGEN-DAZS

20 grammi

**GIULIO MENCARONI**
*ZUCCHERO INVISIBILE, 2012*

Italian information website Il Bureau asked Giulio Mencaroni to create a clear visual about the amount of sugar found in a few foods and drinks. The result: an eye-opening and eye-catching illustration that urges us to rethink certain daily decisions we make concerning our diets.

**RAW COLOR**
*FRANKE ELSHOUT IDENTITY DESIGN, 2012*

Dutch studio Raw Color came up with these business cards for food designer Franke Elshout's corporate identity. The cool pastel colors and simple white outlines perfectly reflect the refined business.

**POST TYPOGRAPHY**
*JOHNS HOPKINS FILM FESTIVAL, 2013*

Johns Hopkins University hosts an annual film festival, and for its 2013 edition, Post Typography designed a hand-drawn poster poking fun at the excess of movie theater concessions, which have become a part of the mainstream cinema experience.

YOU WANT IT?
WE GOT IT!
FILL UP ON A WEEKEND OF FILM
DURING HOPKINS SPRING FAIR!

SHORT FILMS

LOCAL SHORTS

FEATURE FILMS

THE "SINGLE SCREENING" $5

THE "WEEKEND PASS" $20

EVERYTHING ON THE MENU IS FREE WITH YOUR HOPKINS ID!

ALL SCREENINGS

ARE IN SHRIVER HALL

ON THE JHU CAMPUS

(THAT'S THE ONE IN CHARLES VILLAGE)

TAKE A FEW BYTES

STUFF YOURSELF WITH INFORMATION

A SCHEDULE BURSTING AT THE SEAMS

MUTI
ALICE'S ADVENTURES IN WONDERLAND &
HERCULES 2013/2013

When approached about creating an innovative illustration of a classic fairytale, Cape Town-based studio Muti chose Lewis Carroll's **Alice's Adventures in Wonderland.** All of the proceeds from the book in which the illustrations were published went towards fighting illiteracy in Romania. Mingo Lamberti, an exclusive design goods manufacturer in South Africa, also turned to the studio for their creative expertise when needing t-shirt designs for their new "Myths & Legends" range. Muti chose to illustrate an icon set depicting the 12 labors of Hercules.

**DALE EDWIN MURRAY**
*HIP HOP HEADS, 2013*

Tupac and Notorious B.I.G., rap's most famous enemies, are brought together here for Dale Edwin Murray's "Hip Hop Heads." What started as a personal project quickly went viral and has since evolved into an ongoing series. Murray will continue adding to the collection until he's "covered every hip hop great from past to present." An ambitious endeavor that will most certainly delight the numerous fans of the series.

- Bubo Bubo -

- Tyto Alba -

- Asio Otus -

- Otus Scops -

- Nyctea Scandiaca -

- Athene Noctua -

- Strix Nebulosa -

- Strix Aluco -

**ALESSIO SABBADINI**
*OWLS OF THE WORLD, 2012*

Bubo Bubo, Tyto Alba, Nyctea Scandiaca: these words that seem to belong to an enchanting spell are in fact the accurate denominations of various types of owls—who knew scientific names could be so much fun? From the Batman-looking **Otus Scops** to the delicate **Athene Noctua**, Alessio Sabbadini has used clean origami-like lines to design this collection of some of the world's coolest owls.

BURGER KINGDOM

DEBTMARK

IRONY COAST

CAN-ADA

U.S.S.U.V

NOSMOKIA

SPILLED MARTINIQUE

LOBBYNON

EXECUTIVE SALARIA

ECONOMIA

SCAN-DINAVIA

N.R.ASIA

UNITED STATES OF FLORIDA

DENTALIBAN

COCACOLUMBIA

NOWAY

FINLAND

UNITED STATES OF AMNESIA

WORKING OVERTIMOR

"KUWAITER!"

HUNGERY

LA-LA-LAND

SUDANDRUFF

CONFED. OF RUSSIAN NOVELS

**CHRISTOPH NIEMANN**
*THE REAL EMPIRES OF EVIL, 2004*

Commissioned by **Nozone**, an alternative political magazine unafraid of publishing controversial content, this illustration is best described using Christoph Niemann's own words: "I have designed abstract concepts as if they were nation states." We leave it to you to interpret these boldly distorted flags and their equally provocative attributed names.

Editor: Nicholas Blechman

# THE RIGHT SCRUFF

BY GREG HANLON

> A sampling of iconic relief-pitcher facial hair.

**Rollie Fingers, 1968-1985**
THE BARBERSHOP QUARTET: John Thorn, the official historian of Major League Baseball, considers Fingers's mustache the best ever."It looked like Fingers paid attention in the morning," he says.

**Al (The Mad Hungarian) Hrabosky, 1970-1982**
THE FU MANCHU: In 1977, Hrabosky's manager made him shave, and he had his worst year. "The other guys were just cute," he recalls. "I was sick and sinister."

**Rich (Goose) Gossage, 1972-1994**
THE WALRUS: "The most intimidating mustache, I think, was Gossage," says the mustachioed former Met Keith Hernandez. "But it was just a component of his intimidation."

**Dennis Eckersley, 1975-1998**
THE ADULT-FILM STAR: "The blackness and density of that mustache helped him achieve greatness," suggests Aaron Perlut, chairman of the American Mustache Institute.

**Bruce Sutter, 1976-1988**
THE CIVIL WAR GENERAL: "He had a weak chin. He looked better with a beard," Thorn says. Sam Ryan, a reporter for MLB Network, notes, "It was scruffy; it was sloppy; it wasn't well-maintained."

**Lee Smith, 1980-1997**
THE ORIGINAL CHIN STRAP: "He had the Jheri curl working out the back of his hat," says his former teammate Ryne Sandberg. "And then he had the pork-chop sideburns to go with it."

**Eric (Goon) Gagne, 1999-2008**
THE KING TUT: "When guys are appointed closers, they get a starter kit with music and facial hair," says Tom Verducci, the baseball writer.

**Brian Wilson, 2006-PRESENT**
THE RABBI: Wilson, who recently suffered a season-ending elbow injury, is the reigning closer facial-hair king. "You expect to find a flock birds in it," Thorn notes.

**John (The Ax Man) Axford, 2009-PRESENT**
THE WYATT EARP: The American Mustache Institute's 2011 man of the year "should come out of the bullpen wearing chaps," Verducci says.

ILLUSTRATIONS BY CRAIG & KARL

CRAIG & KARL
THE RIGHT SCRUFF 2012

Commissioned by the New York Times for their magazine, "The Right Scruff" depicts nine famous Major League Baseball players and their iconic facial hair, along with hilarious quotes about their scruff.

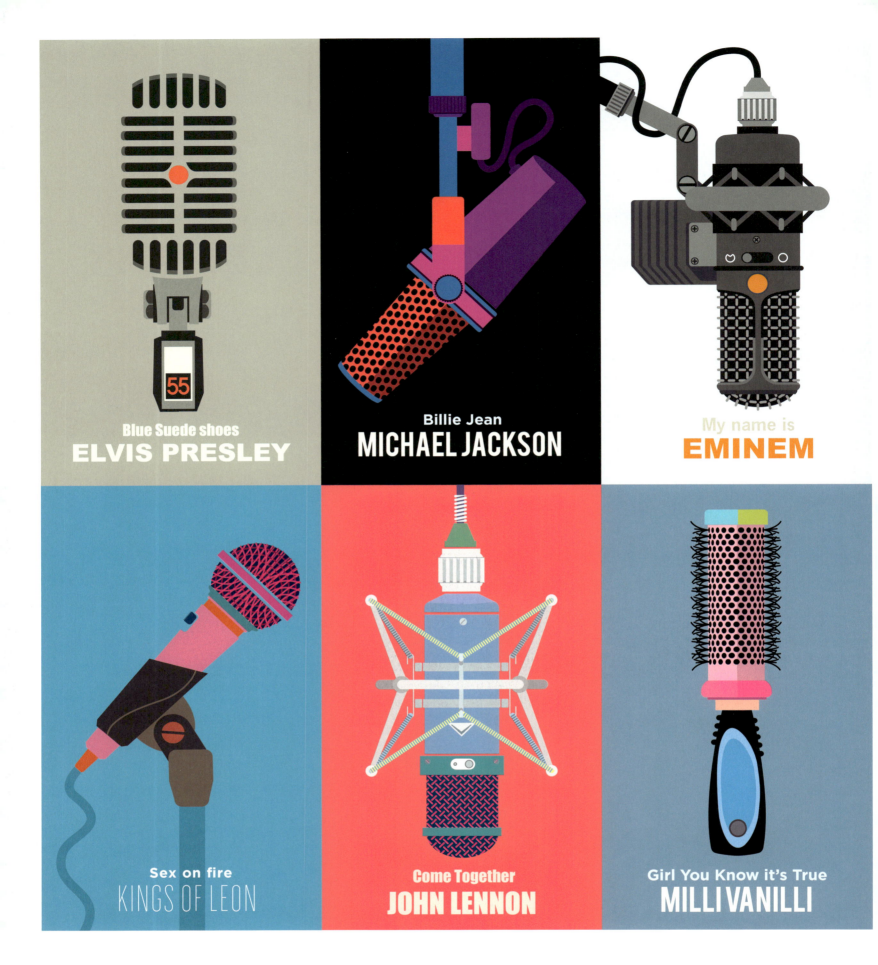

**Blue Suede shoes**
## ELVIS PRESLEY

**Billie Jean**
## MICHAEL JACKSON

**My name is**
## EMINEM

**Sex on fire**
## KINGS OF LEON

**Come Together**
## JOHN LENNON

**Girl You Know it's True**
## MILLI VANILLI

PETER GREENWOOD
*MICROPHONES, 2014*

When investigating the microphones used by famous artists to record iconic pieces of music, Peter Greenwood realized that the microphones themselves are iconic of an era. Using bold graphics and vivid colors, Greenwood then made this illustration, with a humorous twist on the bottom right corner that blends in perfectly with the rest of the microphones.

San Francisco

Johannesburg

New York

Istanbul

Dubai

Tokyo

London

Moscow

Beijing

Sydney

Berlin

Chicago

Buenos Aires

**ROBERT SAMUEL HANSON**
*START UP SPEED, 2012*

Commissioned by the media company The Church of London and published in Google's **Think Quarterly** magazine, this illustration is about maintaining a successful start-up company's nimble quality and reasonable rising speed as it expands.

**ANDREA MANZATI**
*STUFF ON WHITE BACKGROUND, 2010*

Don't let the name of this print fool you—Italian graphic designer and illustrator Andrea Manzati knows exactly what he's doing. The so-called "stuff" is in fact everything you can expect to find on Manzati's desk on any given day, along with a few extra items that might be lying around, such as an old-school Game Boy or Polaroid camera. The neat composition and textured objects reflect Manzati's signature design style.

**DANIEL NYARI**
*FAMOUS WEAPONS, 2012*

Some are amusing while others are quite scary: the range of weapons illustrated on this print by Daniel Nyari all stem from contemporary popular culture. These famous weapons are the most recognizable gadgets associated with the pop protagonists who carry them. After all, what would Frodo be without the One Ring? Or Freddy Krueger without his clawed leather glove? And Super Mario would definitely not be the same without his Koopa Troopa shells!

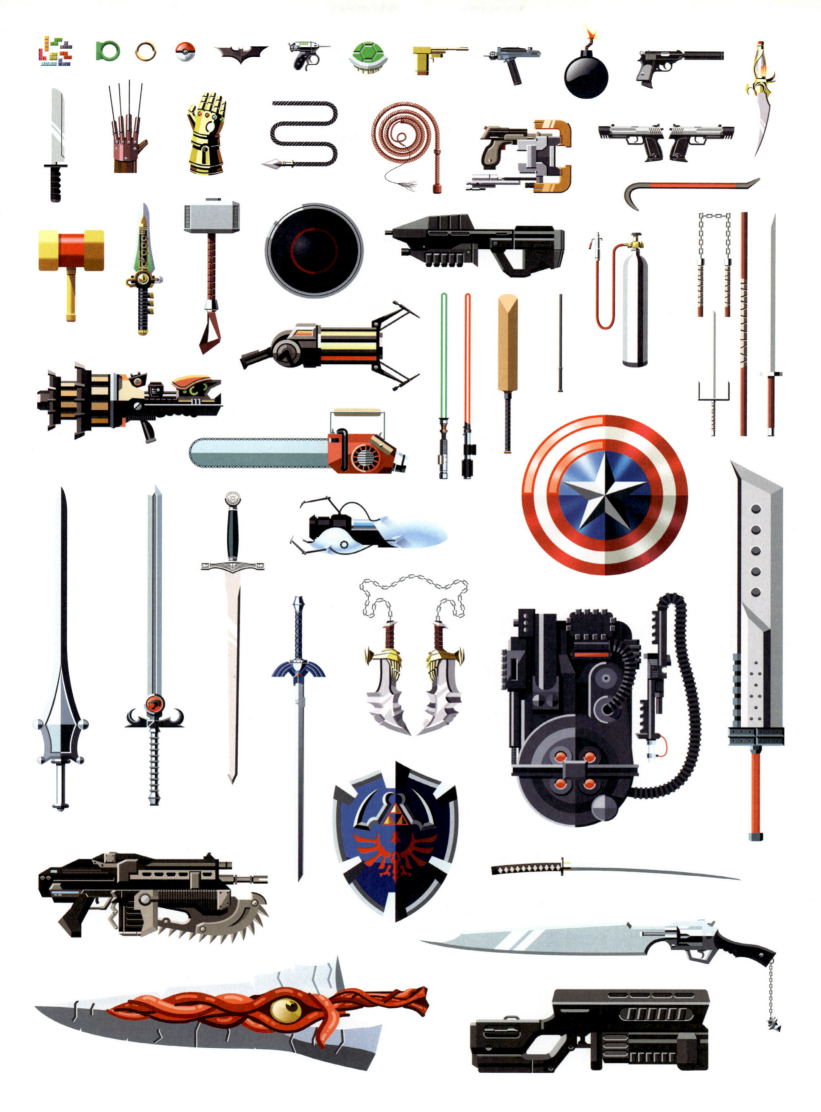

# FAMOUS
# WEAPONS

TETRIMINOS, *TETRIS* POWER RING, *GREEN LANTERN* THE ONE RING, *LORD OF THE RINGS* POKE BALL, *POKEMON* BATARANG, *BATMAN* NOISY CRICKET, *MEN IN BLACK* KOOPA TROOPA SHELL, *SUPER MARIO BROS.* PHASER PISTOL, *STAR TREK SERIES*
GOLDEN GUN, *MAN WITH THE GOLDEN GUN* BOMB, *BOMBERMAN* WALTHER PPK, *JAMES BOND SERIES* DAGGER OF TIME, *PRINCE OF PERSIA* MACHETE, *FRIDAY THE 13TH SERIES*, CLAWED LEATHER GLOVE, *NIGHTMARE ON ELM STREET SERIES*
INFINITY GAUNTLET, *MARVEL COMICS* SCORPION'S SPEAR, *MORTAL KOMBAT* WHIP, *INDIANA JONES SERIES* PLASMA CUTTER, *DEAD SPACE SERIES* H&K USP MATCH X 2, *TOMB RAIDER SERIES* CROWBAR, *HALF-LIFE SERIES* HAMMER, *DONKEY KONG*
DRAGON DAGGER, *POWER RANGERS* MJOLNIR, *MARVEL COMICS* BLADE RIMMED HAT, *MORTAL KOMBAT* MA 37, *HALO SERIES* CAPTIVE BOLT PISTOL, *NO COUNTRY FOR OLD MEN* KATANA, NUNCHAKU, BO, SAI, *TEENAGE MUTANT NINJA TURLES*
RYNO V, *RATCHET & CLANK: A CRACK IN TIME* GRAVITY GUN, *HALF-LIFE 2* LIGHTSABERS, *STAR WARS SERIES* CRICKET BAT, *SHAUN OF THE DEAD* WAND, *HARRY POTTER SERIES* CHAINSAW, *THE TEXAS CHAINSAW MASSACRE, EVIL DEAD SERIES*
THE POWER SWORD, *MASTERS OF THE UNIVERSE* SWORD OF OMENS, *THUNDERCATS* EXCALIBUR, *ARTHURIAN LEGEND* PORTAL GUN, *PORTAL SERIES* CAPTAIN AMERICA SHIELD, *MARVEL COMICS* MASTER SWORD & SHIELD, *LEGEND OF ZELDA SERIES*
DOUBLE-CHAINED BLADES, *GOD OF WAR SERIES* PROTON PACK, *GHOSTBUSTERS SERIES* BUSTER SWORD, *FINAL FANTASY VII* MK 2 LANCER ASSAULT RIFLE, *GEARS OF WAR SERIES* HATTORI HANZO, *KILL BILL SERIES* GUN BLADE, *FINAL FANTASY VIII*
SOUL EDGE, *SOUL CALIBUR SERIES* BFG 9000, *DOOM SERIES* © DANIEL NYARI, 2012

# A Short History of
# PHOTOGRAPHIC
# CAMERA

*by Retro-futurismo Kitsch.*

**X Century a.c.**
Camera Obscura

**1835**
Talbot's Mousetrap

**1839**
Giroux Camera

**1841**
Voigtländer
Daguerreotype Camera

**1853**
Archer Camera

**1856**
Captain Fowke
Camera

**1856**
Dancer Binocular
Daguerreotype Camera

**1860**
Dubroni

**1862**
Johnson & Harrison
Pantoscopic Camera

**1862**
Thompson
Revolver Camera

**1885**
Stirn
Vest Camera

**1888**
Kodak

**1889**
Luzo

**1889**
Demon Detective

**1889**
L'Escopette

**1890**
Frena

**1895**
Folding
Pocket Kodak

**1900**
Brownie

**1904**
Ticka

**1909**
Soho Tropical Reflex

**1912**
Aptus

**1912**
Vest Pocket Kodak

**1912**
Speed Graphic

**1924**
Ermanox

**1924**
Jos-Pe

**1925**
Leica

**1928**
Beau Brownie

**1928**
Retina

**1929**
Rolleiflex

**1933**
Polyfoto

**1936**
Kine Exakta

**1937**
Minox

**1938**
Super Kodak Six-20

**1942**
Kodak Baby
Brownie

**1947**
Stereo Realist

**1948**
Polaroid Land 95

**1949**
Canon IIB

**1959**
Nikon F

**1959**
Olympus Pen

**1962**
Hasselblad
Lunar Surface

**1963**
Kodak Instamatic 50

**1965**
Graph-check
Sequence Camera

**1966**
Rollei 35

**1972**
Polaroid SX 70

**1976**
Minolta 110 Zoom
SLR

**1978**
Polaroid
Supercolor 600

**1978**
Kodak Colorburst 100
Instant Camera

**1981**
Sony Mavica

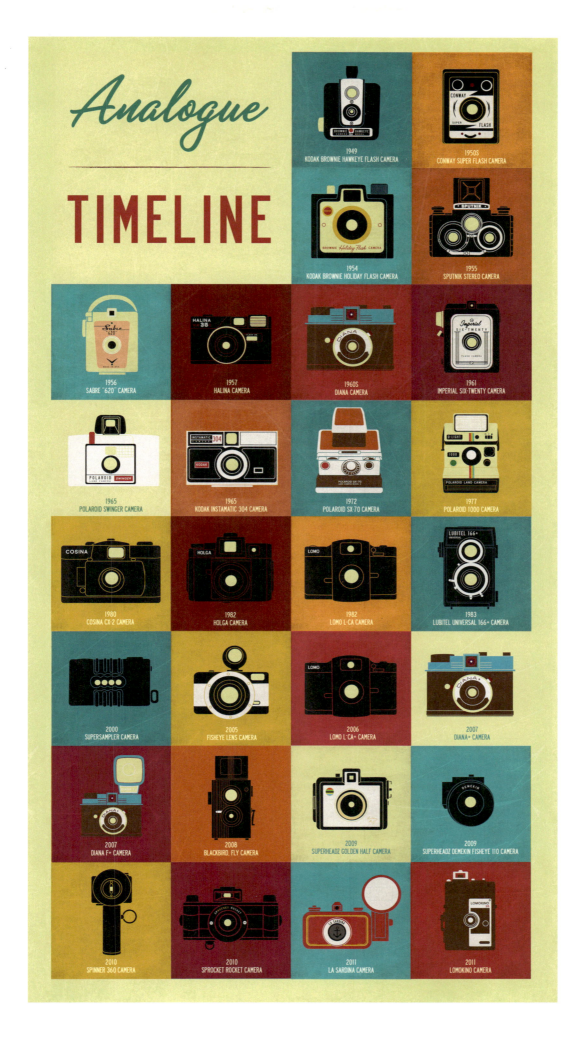

# Analogue

# TIMELINE

**1949**
KODAK BROWNIE HAWKEYE FLASH CAMERA

**1950S**
CONWAY SUPER FLASH CAMERA

**1954**
KODAK BROWNIE HOLIDAY FLASH CAMERA

**1955**
SPUTNIK STEREO CAMERA

**1956**
SABRE "620" CAMERA

**1957**
HALINA CAMERA

**1960S**
DIANA CAMERA

**1961**
IMPERIAL SIX-TWENTY CAMERA

**1965**
POLAROID SWINGER CAMERA

**1965**
KODAK INSTAMATIC 304 CAMERA

**1972**
POLAROID SX-70 CAMERA

**1977**
POLAROID 1000 CAMERA

**1980**
COSINA CX-2 CAMERA

**1982**
HOLGA CAMERA

**1982**
LOMO L-CA CAMERA

**1983**
LUBITEL UNIVERSAL 166+ CAMERA

**2000**
SUPERSAMPLER CAMERA

**2005**
FISHEYE LENS CAMERA

**2006**
LOMO L'CA+ CAMERA

**2007**
DIANA+ CAMERA

**2007**
DIANA F+ CAMERA

**2008**
BLACKBIRD, FLY CAMERA

**2009**
SUPERHEADZ GOLDEN HALF CAMERA

**2009**
SUPERHEADZ DEMEKIN FISHEYE 110 CAMERA

**2010**
SPINNER 360 CAMERA

**2010**
SPROCKET ROCKET CAMERA

**2011**
LA SARDINA CAMERA

**2011**
LOMOKINO CAMERA

**RETRO-FUTURISMO KITSCH**
*A SHORT HISTORY OF PHOTOGRAPHIC CAMERA, 2014*

This print is a visual compendium of the most notable photographic cameras throughout history. These cameras were selected for their technical advances or for their historical relevance, starting with the camera obscura and ending with the Sony Mavica, considered the first commercial camera of the digital era.

**NICOLE TAN**
*ANALOGUE TIMELINE, 2012*

A visual timeline showing the evolution of analog cameras throughout the years, this illustration was featured in **Blackbird,** a magazine that focuses on toy cameras and everything analog.

# THE CYCLISTS
## - MEET THEM ALL -

- MRS. CUBEBRICK & DOG -

- SIR HUMPTY STUMPY -

- MR. ARACHNID -

- MR. STILTS -

- DR. NOPADDLE -

- THE TANDEMO SISTERS -

- FRANK THE FLEA -

**JACQUES & LISE**
*MEET THE CYCLISTS & BANANAZ, 2012*

The illustration "Meet the Cyclists" showcases different fictitious characters matched with various types of vintage bicycles. When the graphic designers Jacques & Lise saw a high-wheeled bicycle in a museum, they playfully imagined what a person riding such a bike would look like. Therefore, people riding a tandem bike have to be Siamese twins and a man riding the high-wheeled bike can indeed only have very long legs. Just as playful as the cyclists are the banana-shaped thoughts that apes may have about world problems, dreams, and desires.

**ANGRYBLUE**
*WEAPONS OF MASS CREATION, 2011-2013*

Make art, not war: these screen prints by Angryblue (a.k.a. Justin Kamerer) compile mass-produced tools needed to make music, fine art, and film, and place them within the outlines of destructive weapons.

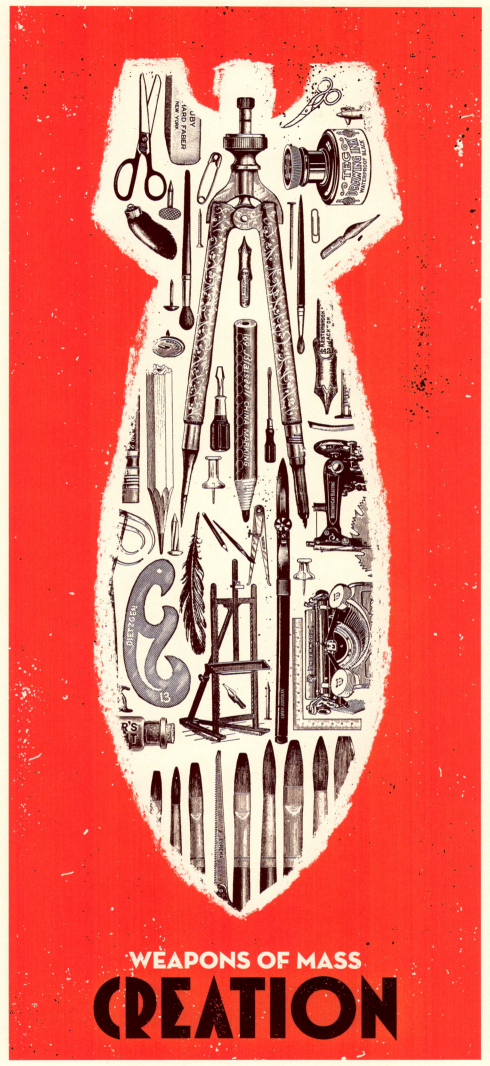

WEAPONS OF MASS
CREATION

DESIGN BY ANGRYBLUE - PRINTED AT CRACKHEAD PRESS IN LOUISVILLE, KY

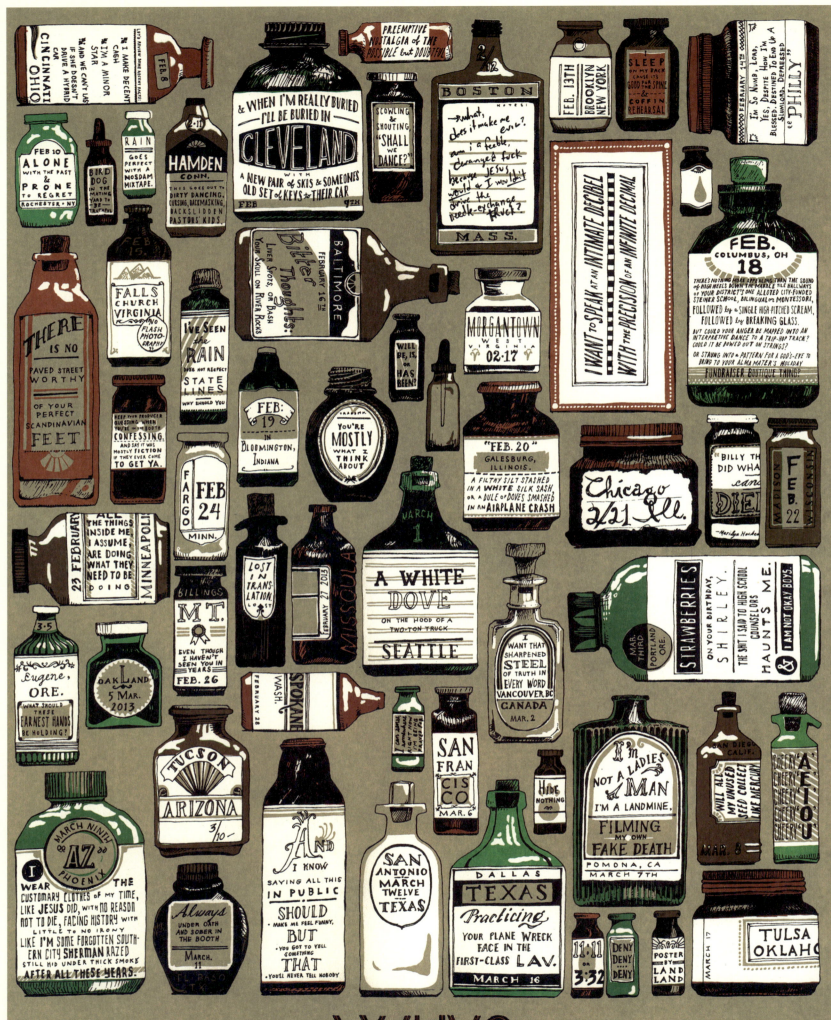

**LANDLAND**
*WHY? TOUR POSTER, 2013*

This four-color screen print designed by very-small-but-very-capable two-person studio Landland is not your run-of-the-mill tour poster. For alternative hip hop and indie rock band WHY?, Landland came up with a personalized image that includes many of the band's lyrics on container labels.

**KYLER MARTZ**
*DRUNK AGAIN, 2013*

This print by Seattle-based illustrator Kyler Martz is inspired by liquor cabinets and bar walls. Martz coyly plays on various brands of liquor and old drinking adages to create original imagery for the bottled alcohol designs.

MUTI

*SOUTHERN COMFORT, 2013*

This print was made for the Southern Comfort Creative Exchange competition in 2013. The theme was to create an illustration that captured the spirit of Mardi Gras in New Orleans.

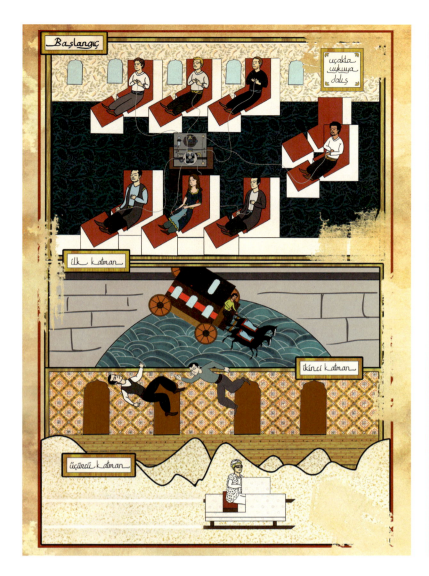

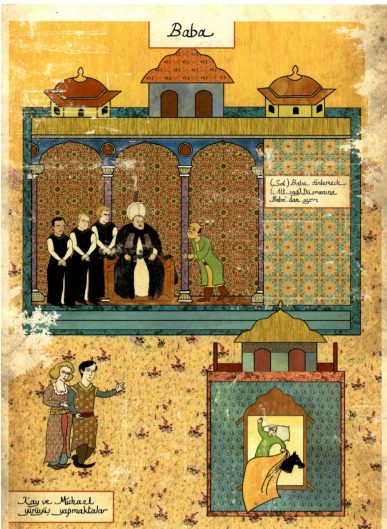

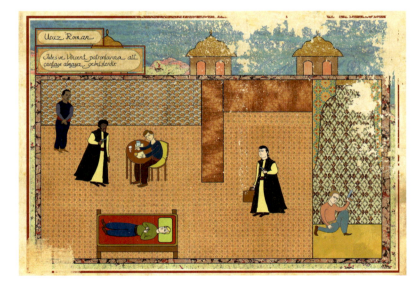

## MURAT PALTA
*OTTOMAN STYLE FILM POSTERS, 2010-2012*

Turkish illustrator Murat Palta transforms iconic scenes from contemporary cult classic films into Ottoman-era-style miniature paintings. On the page to the left, the poster for **A Clockwork Orange** can be found at the top and **Kill Bill** at the bottom. On this page, **Inception** is on the top left, **The Godfather** on the top right, **Pulp Fiction** on the bottom left, and **Goodfellas** on the bottom right.

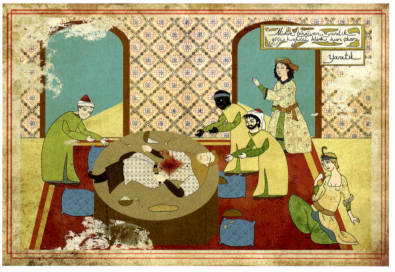

**MURAT PALTA**
*OTTOMAN STYLE FILM POSTERS, 2010-2012*

More Ottoman-era-style posters of contemporary film classics by Istanbul-based Murat Palta. **Star Wars** is illustrated at the top to the left, **Scarface** is next to it on the right, and **Terminator** and **Alien** are at the bottom, respectively. On the next page, the poster for **The Shining** can be found.

**MARTIN JARRIE**
*MA CARTE DE VOEUX 2013, 2013*

French painter and illustrator Martin Jarrie was inspired by catalogs and encyclopedias from the Enlightenment period when designing this card to celebrate the New Year in 2013. An original way of wishing "Bonne Année!" to friends and family.

figure V

···FUNGI···

**VLADIMIR STANKOVIC**
*FUNGI & CEPHALOPODOPTERA, 2012/2014*

"Fungi" and "Cephalopodoptera" are personal projects by Serbian illustrator Vladimir Stankovic. The first print shows various unusual fungi species in the manner of vintage nature encyclopedias, and the second depicts a peculiar species between a mollusk and an insect. Stankovic enlightens us on the matter and explains that "these creatures live in the deepest underwater caves of oceans worldwide. With similar intelligence and characteristics of moths, beetles, octopuses, and squids, these animals have managed to remain hidden for centuries."

1.

2.

3.

4.

5.

6.

7.

Lycopodon Giganteum
Flora of the Secondary Period

sigillaria's asterophyllites

**KATIE SCOTT**
*FLOATING TERRARIUMS & MUSHROOM,
2012/2011*

Katie Scott describes "Floating Terrariums" as "a fantasy vision of terrariums and plant life," which she designed as a personal project. "Mushroom," a hand-drawn print digitally colored using watercolor swatches, was inspired by Jules Verne's **Journey to the Center of the Earth.**

**KATIE SCOTT**
*SOIL, 2013*

Soil is the foundation on which terrestrial biodiversity is built. Without a varied ecosystem, the world's food chain would be disrupted. Through her drawings, Katie Scott explores biological hybridization, particularly within human anatomy and botanical life forms. The illustration was commissioned to accompany an article published in the **New York Times**'s Sunday Review about the biodiversity of soil, seeking to demonstrate the surprising extent to which the matter under our feet is complex.

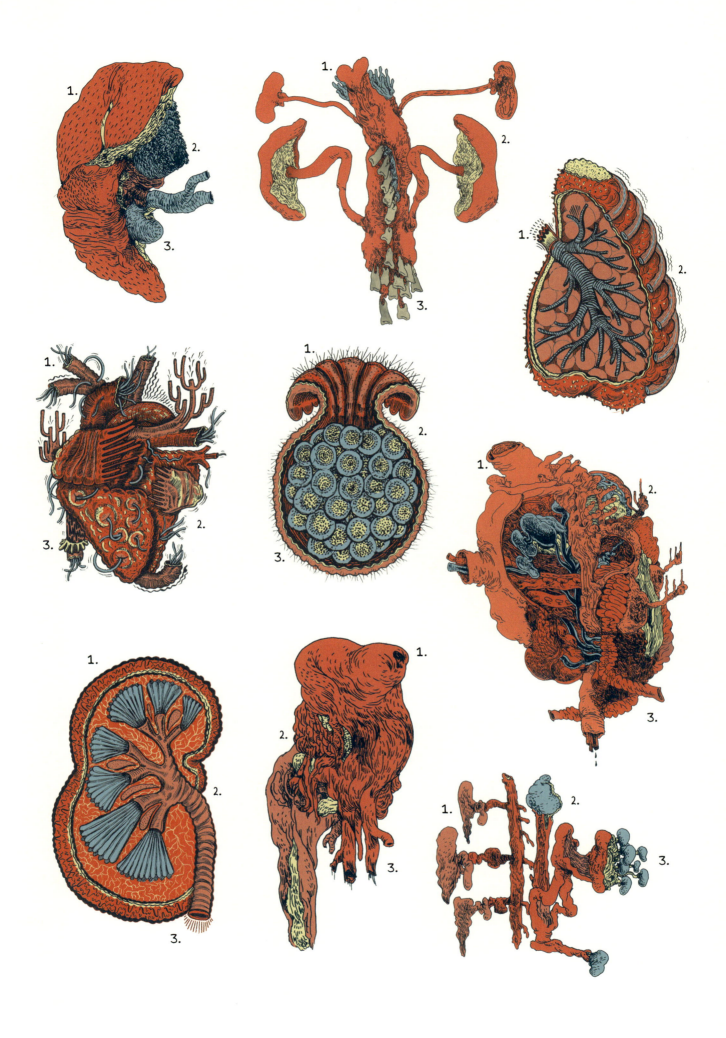

**ERIK SVETOFT**
*ORGANS, 2013*

Swedish artist and illustrator Erik Svetoft has a way with lines. His style is reminiscent of medieval engravings and is often raw, with a slightly grotesque touch. For this illustration, Svetoft teamed up with textile designer Llew Mejia. The collection shows lesser-known human organs that are often overlooked in anatomy books. On these drawings, Svetoft's distinctive strokes conjure images from underwater scenery.

KATIE SCOTT
*BARNABÉ FILLION PARFUMS, 2013*

Katie Scott worked together with French perfume designer Barnabé Fillion to create these alchemy-inspired illustrations for the perfumery's corporate identity.

SOUTH CAROLINA

MINNESOTA

CONNECTICUT

INDIANA

COLORADO

CALIFORNIA

ARKANSAS

WASHINGTON

ARIZONA

ALASKA

ALABAMA

OREGON

MICHIGAN

KENTUCKY

**LUCY ENGELMAN**
*BIRD-TREE-FLOWER, 2013*

"Bird-Tree-Flower" was inspired by Lucy Engelman's love of nature, and is a unique way of representing a few U.S. states as well as celebrating their flora and fauna.

MUTI
*LITTLE WHITE LIES 50TH EDITION*

Little White Lies is a bi-monthly British independent movie magazine that features writing, illustration, and photography related to cinema. They celebrated their 50th issue with 50 writers and 50 artists illustrating 50 of the best films from the past 50 years. South African studio MUTI was invited to create an illustration for Wes Anderson's Moonrise Kingdom for the occasion. The illustration was also shown in London's 71a gallery during the "Project Fifty" exhibition.

360° of Cake

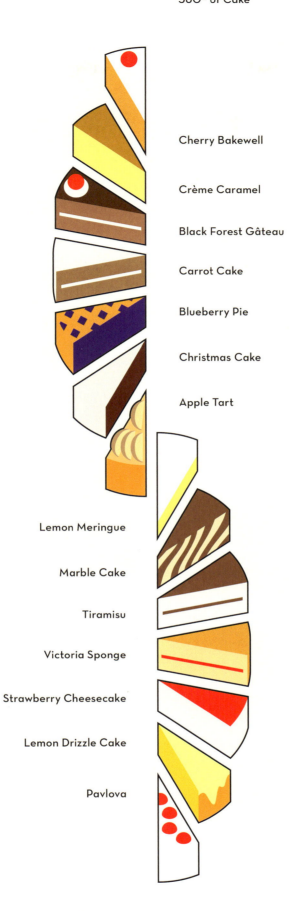

Cherry Bakewell

Crème Caramel

Black Forest Gâteau

Carrot Cake

Blueberry Pie

Christmas Cake

Apple Tart

Lemon Meringue

Marble Cake

Tiramisu

Victoria Sponge

Strawberry Cheesecake

Lemon Drizzle Cake

Pavlova

**BURLESQUE
OF NORTH AMERICA**
*BONNAROO MUSIC & ARTS FESTIVAL, 2009*

Bon Iver is represented as a snowflake, Nine Inch Nails as a huge hammer, and Public Enemy as a clock. For the 2009 edition of the Bonnaroo Music & Arts Festival in Manchester, Tennessee, designer Mike Davis and screen printer Ben LaFond from Minneapolis-based Burlesque of North America created a concert poster where each headlining artist is represented by an illustration. The drawings refer to the name of the act, one of their songs, some inside joke for their fans, or their overall spirit.

**LINUS KRAEMER**
*360 DEGREES OF CAKE, 2010*

When London-based illustrator Linus Kraemer couldn't decide what kind of birthday cake to make for his friend's birthday, he explains, he created an exploded pie chart of all the kinds of cake he could think of, and designed "the slices with equal size to allow for a fair and unbiased decision." The fact that Kraemer has a degree in engineering mathematics probably has something to do with it.

# THE A-Z

ALPHA & OMEGA

DENNIS BOVELL

CYBERDUB

DIGI-DUB

ECHO CHAMBER

PRINCE FAR-I

WALTER GIBBONS

KEITH HUDSON

IMAGINATION

JAH SHAKA

KING TUBBY

LATIN HIPHOP

MAD PROFESSOR

NU GROOVE

ON-U SOUND

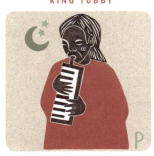

AUGUSTUS PABLO

QAWWALI DUB

ARTHUR RUSSELL

SCIENTIST

TRICKY

THE UPSETTER

VIRTUAL DUB

WARRIORS DANCE

X-RAY

YAMAHA SKANK

ZOE

# OF DUB

## SOPHIE BASS
*THE A-Z OF DUB MUSIC, 2013*

In 1994, music writer David Toop wrote an article for **The Wire** magazine in which he alphabetized a list of dub music's most vital players. Sophie Bass's two loves are music and art, so when she decided to create a poster as an homage to dub music, she knew where to turn. Bass describes the process as having been satisfying, as the medium forced her to summarize and organize an extensive topic into 26 key elements. She adds that "using the woodcuts and naïve art from Africa and the Caribbean as visual inspiration, the piece became as playful and exciting as the music it speaks of." The artistic collaboration between Toop and Bass was taken to the next step as "The A-Z Of Dub Music" was turned into a book of the same name.

**THE A TO Zs OF EXTINCT AND ENDANGERED ANIMALS.**
SAVING THE REMAINING ISN'T AS EASY AS ABC. SUPPORT WILDLIFE CONSERVATION. LEARN MORE ON NATGEO WILD.

**NAT GEO WILD**

Agency: Kinetic Singapore | Creative Director: Pann Lim | Art Director: Elen Winata | Illustrator: Elen Winata | Copywriter: Eugene Tan | Account Director: Daniel Tan

**ELEN WINATA**
*NATIONAL GEOGRAPHIC A-Z*

commissioned by NatGeo Wild, Elen Winata has created an original, informative alphabet of extinct and endangered animals starting with the addax and ending with the zebra duiker.

ANATOMY OF A FEMALE CHICKEN

1. Brain.
2. Ear.
3. Vertebrae of the backbone.
4. Full extent of the left lung.
5. Spleen.
6. Ovaries.
7. Left kidney.
8. Caeca.
9. Oviduct.
10. Cloaca.
11. Large intestine.
12. Small intestine.
13. Pancreas.
14. Gizzard.
15. Liver.
16. Proventriculus.
17. The heart.
18. Crop.
19. Trachea.
20. Oesophagus.

## HATCHING AN EGG

### FERTILE OR INFERTILE

Eggs which are to be eaten should be collected daily from the chickens coop soon after laying. A fertile egg is safe for human consumption, just like an infertile one.

Fertile eggs will only develop an embryo (visible after 3 days) when they are left in a favourable warm environment, either under a broody hen or in an incubator with a constant temperature of 37.5°C.

**DAY 2**
Blood vessels will be evident, the vertebral column will begin to form and early tissue development will be visible.

**DAY 5**
Along with the appearance of elbows and knees, the heart will have started beating, eye pigmentation has also begun.

**DAY 10**
The formation of the beak and comb has started, feather tracts are visible and the embryo takes on a bird like appearance.

**DAY 14**
Tail feathers will be evident along with scales and toes, the embryo will have turned its head towards the large end of the egg.

**DAY 18**
Feathers will now cover the body, the head will have moved under the right wing, the growth of the embryo is now nearly complete.

**DAY 21**
With the embryo fully formed, the chick is now ready to hatch and break free from the shell, this process can take 4-12 hours.

### CHICKS

Hatching is one of the most demanding and dangerous times in any birds life. The shell is built to be strong and its sharp edges and internal layers can make hatching a hazardous process.

The warm temperature the chicks are used to during incubation must be maintained after hatching, the best way to do this is with the use of a heat lamp suspended above the chicks until they are 'feathered up'.

## REARING POULTRY

### HENHOUSE & ENVIRONMENT

Ample room to perch and nest is good for a chicken. Access to fertile ground appeals to their foraging instincts, this allows for a balanced diet of seeds, snails, worms, bugs and grass. They should also receive a regular feed of natural cereals.

### THE COCK

Along with providing a hen with fertile eggs during the mating process, a cockerel will also contribute to the social cohesion of a female flock, he will keep the peace amongst the competing hens and also call them to richer food sources.

### MOTHER HEN

A chicken can lay an egg every 1-2 days, this can be done without mating a cockerel. If she has mated, she will lay fertile eggs within 2 weeks.

A broody hen will sit continuously on a clutch of eggs for 21 days or more, this is the natural incubation period. For hens that don't go broody, a surrogate 'broodie' can be used to sit on and incubate other hens eggs.

### THE PREDATOR

To lose one chicken to a fox attack is bad, to lose an entire flock is devastating. Night time and early morning are the biggest dangers, a level of freedom is important, but a safe henhouse with secure boundaries will help mitigate the danger.

## THE CHICKEN

A chicken should have reached full maturity of at least 80 days before eating. Weight will vary depending on the breed, a leggy bird with small breasts delivers flavoursome meat, whereas a large breasted bird will produce more lean white meat.

**1. WISHBONE**
Traditionally snapped at the dinner table.

**2. OYSTER**
Two oval discs of sweet brown meat.

**3. WING**
Brown meat, sometimes marinated to enhance flavour.

**4. BREAST**
Mild tasting, lean white meat with no bones.

**5. THIGH**
A dark meat, rich in flavour, retains moisture well.

**6. PARSONS NOSE**
Sweet and tender delicacy from the rear of the bird.

**7. DRUMSTICK**
Part of the leg, the meat is very similar to the thigh.

**8. FEET**
Chewy texture comprising of skin and tendons.

**GIBLETS**
Consists of the heart, liver and gizzard.

## THE EGG

A busy domestic chicken can lay more than 300 eggs a year. Eggs are the cornerstone to many a breakfast. They are also used in countless recipes, their propensity to bind, thicken, emulsify and set means they are indispensable when cooking and baking.

**SOFT BOILED**
Traditionally dipped with toasted bread soldiers.

**BAKING**
Eggs mixed with flour, butter, sugar, milk and baking soda.

**OMELETTE & SCRAMBLED**
Omelettes comprise of an egg mixed with savoury items. The only addition to scramble is milk.

**QUICHE & FLAN**
Eggs whisked with milk along with sweet or savoury ingredients.

**SCOTCH EGG**
Egg is hard boiled, wrapped in sausage meat and coated in bread crumbs.

**POACHED**
If cooked without apparatus, vinegar can be used in water to help bind the egg.

**FRIED**
This requires good technique, egg must be cooked under medium to high heat.

## KILLING A CHICKEN

Ideally a chicken is killed at between 80 and 155 days, this will be dependent on the birds weight, along with its breed and individuality. In order to reduce distress amongst the rest of the flock, the chosen chicken should be removed from the vicinity of its fellows before it is killed.

**WRINGING THE NECK**
With the snapping of neck vertebrae, there should be an audible click, in some instances the head may come off if the exertion is too strong.

**THE CHOP**
A very sharp hatchet is required, this technique can be very distressing and is neither the quickest or kindest way for a chicken to die.

**THE CONE**
A cone will eliminate the flapping of wings, the point of entry for the knife is the beak, the knife is then twisted upon entering the skull area.

**PLUCKING**
A chicken should be bled as soon as its been killed, plucking should then commence, if left the feathers will become tight and harden in the skin.

~ Figures of Surrealism ~

Top Row: Antonin Artaud / Elsa Schiaparelli / Man Ray / Paul Eluard.   Second Row: Marcel Duchamp / Hans Bellmer / Rene Magritte / Meret Oppenheim.   Third Row: Luis Bunuel / Philippe Soupault / Max Ernst / Sigmund Freud.   Fourth Row: Giorgio de Chirico / Salvador Dali / Valentine Hugo / Andre Breton.   Bottom Row: Gala Eluard (Dali) / Yves Tanguy / Alberto Giacometti / Joan Miro.

**IAN MCDONNELL**
*THE CHICKEN OR THE EGG, 2013*

Not to be mistaken for an attempt to shed light on the age-old question about which came first, "The Chicken or the Egg" is in fact a humorously informative print that looks at the life cycle of a chicken in today's society, touching on topics such as egg fertility, feather plucking, and egg hatching.

**ROBBIE PORTER**
*FIGURES OF SURREALISM, 2012*

Designer Robbie Porter describes this piece as "a surreal re-working of the surrealists themselves," and explains that he "wanted each member to have a surreal context. For example, Magritte is invisible with the iconic bowler hat still in frame, the fashion designer Elsa Schiaparelli has leopard print skin, and Dali is dreaming."

161

RACISM
ERASES
FACE

Bruce Willen 2002

## POST TYPOGRAPHY
*RACISM ERASES FACE, 2002*

When asked to create a public service poster for the city of Baltimore on the subject of race relations, Post Typography decided to take Polaroid pictures of its diverse group of friends and acquaintances and blank out their faces. A poignant piece, "Racism Erases Face" speaks to the way in which racism strips people of their individuality in favor of ignorant generalizations.

## FEDERICO BABINA
*ARCHIST, 2014*

Ingeniously transforming famous painters into architects, Italian illustrator Federico Babina imagined what a house by Dalí or a museum designed by Miró would look like. Babina explains, "These images represent a world of shapes that use the brush to paint architecture."

# ARCHIST CITY

JACK PALANCE

DOLPH LUNDGREN

CLINT EASTWOOD

UMA THURMAN

KIRK DOUGLA

WESLEY SNIPES

SYLVESTER STALLONE

30 HOLLY HARD

CHARLES BRONSON

CHUCK NORRIS

ARNOLD SCHWARZ-ENEGGER

SIGOURNEY WEAVER

HARVEY KEITEL

CARL WEATHERS

ROBERT MITCHUM

SAMUEL JACKSON

**MARIO ZUCCA**
*30 HOLLYWOOD HARDASSES, 2013*

A series of portraits of Hollywood tough-guys (and girls) specifically made for a group exhibition in Pittsburgh called "Craft Hard: Art Inspired by Action Movies."

MICKEY ROURKE

STEVE McQUEEN

VIN DIESEL

JOHN WAYNE

ROBERT DENIRO

BRUCE LEE

JEAN CLAUDE VAN DAMME

LINDA HAMILTON

OOD

SSES

DAVID CARRADINE

GENE HACKMAN

KURT RUSSELL

LEE MARVIN

DWAYNE JOHNSON

PAM GRIER

BRUCE WILLIS

These 30 portraits were done by Mario Zucca for the four-person group exhibition *Craft Hard: Art Inspired by Action Movies*. The show runs from June 6 – June 22, 2013 at Wildcard in Pittsburgh, PA.

ELISABETH
OF YORK

CATHERINE
OF ARAGON

ANNE BOLEYN

JANE SEYMOUR

ANNE OF CLEVES

CATHERINE
HOWARD

CATHERINE PARR

JANE GREY

MARY TUDOR

ELISABETH I.

ANNE OF DENMARK

HENRIETTA MARIA
OF FRANCE

CATHERINE
OF BRAGANZA

MARY OF MODENA

MARY II.

ANNE

SOPHIE DOROTHEA
OF BRUNSWICK

CAROLINE OF
ANSBACH

CHARLOTTE OF
MECKLENBURG-STRELITZ

CAROLINE OF
BRUNSWICK

ADELAIDE OF
SAXE-MEININGEN

VICTORIA

ALEXANDRA
OF DENMARK

MARY OF TECK

ELISABETH
BOWES-LYON

ELISABETH II.

## KATJA SPITZER

Katja Spitzer created the original screen print poster "26 Queens of England" in 2009 for her diploma at the Academy of Visual Arts. The print was then featured in Quodlibet: A Q-Rated Encyclopaedia, a book containing 26 items that begin with the letter Q. Inspired by Georges Perec, who is famous for having written a book whose sole subject was the letter E, Spitzer and writer Sebastian Gievert teamed up to tackle the letter Q.

**PETER OUMANSKI**
*CLASSICAL STRUGGLES AT DIGITAL, 2011*

Like many other genres, classical music lost its primary retail home when brick-and-mortar fell. But unlike others, it had to face significant boundaries when entering the subsequent digital age: a tremendous back catalog, a taxonomy unfriendly to search, and a graying fan base. For a fun take on this theme, Peter Oumanski illustrated famous composers confused by MP3 players. The print was commissioned by **Billboard**—one of the oldest trade magazines in the world, first published in 1894. While Chopin and Prokofiev are seriously distracted by headphone wires, Stravinsky simply smashes the sinister gadget with his foot.

SCOTT C
*GREAT SHOWDOWNS, 2013*

This illustration is a small selection from a larger series of pivotal moments from a variety of famous films such as **Star Wars** and **Grease**. The entirety of the "Great Showdowns" series, which includes intense moments beyond film history, was turned into two books, **Great Showdowns** and **Great Showdowns: The Return**.

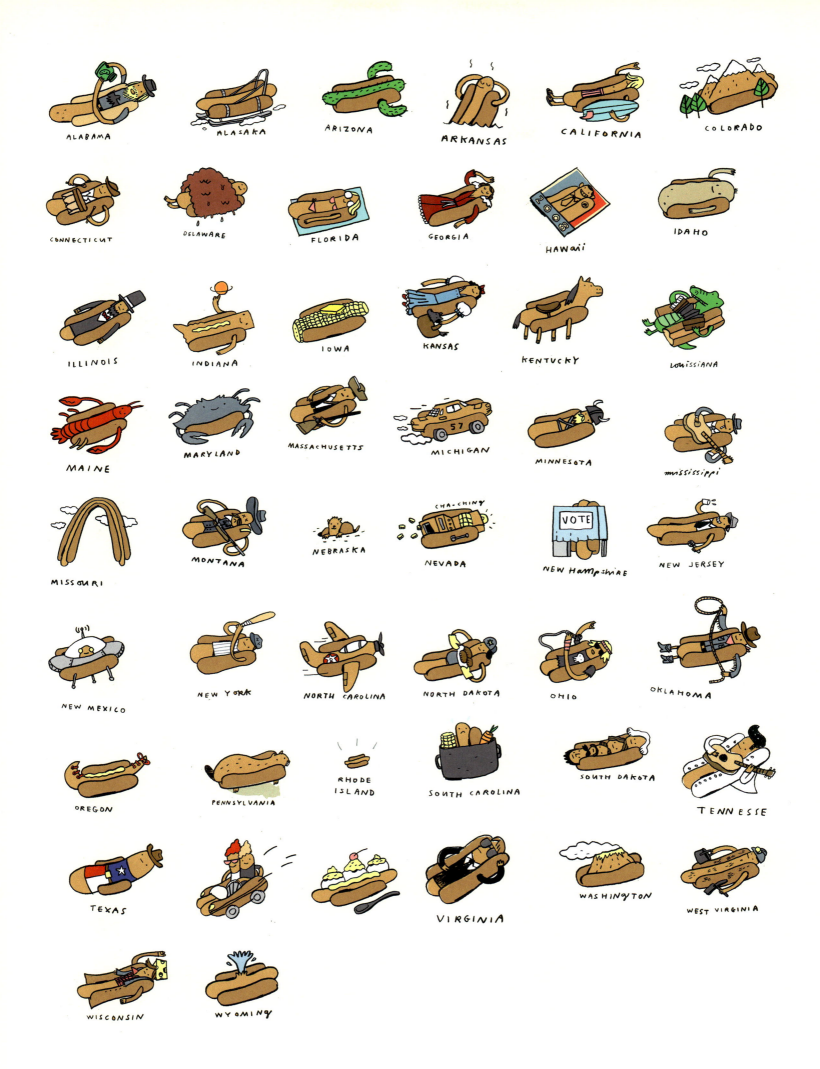

**MIKE LOWERY**
*HOT DOGS OF THE UNITED STATES, 2012*

Commissioned by Peter Mayer Advertising for a promotion piece, Mike Lowery was asked to make a map of the United States with hot dogs representing each of the 50 states.

**ATHERTON LIN**
*COUNTRIES OF THE WORLD, 2011*

Between 2009 and 2012, life partners Jamie Atherton and Jeremy Atherton Lin collaborated on a project producing narrative-based paper goods. One of the items created under the Atherton Lin moniker was a travelogue for which "Countries of the World" was originally designed as endpapers. "Countries of the World" was developed from original watercolor drawings of the shapes of all the world's states and territories, which amounted to 230 at the time. The drawings were then reduced to equal dimensions and arranged in order of area. Patterns emerge. Larger countries retain some of the complexity of their coastlines and borders, whereas some city-states become soft and amoeba-like.

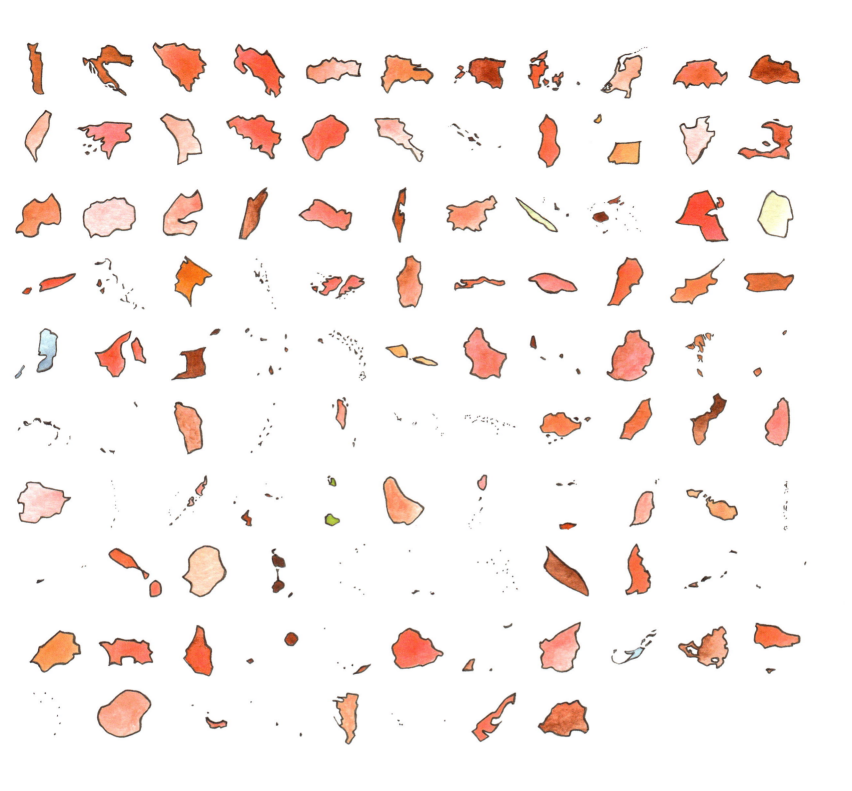

©ATHERTON LIN

**JULIA ROTHMAN**
*VEGETABLE CHART & FARM CHART, 2012*

From tractors and pigs to crop rotation patterns and all sorts of vegetables, Julia Rothman has created an entertaining and informative picture of country life. The illustrations are part of Rothman's book **Farm Anatomy: The Curious Parts and Pieces of Country Life**, which reveals fascinating facts about rural living.

172

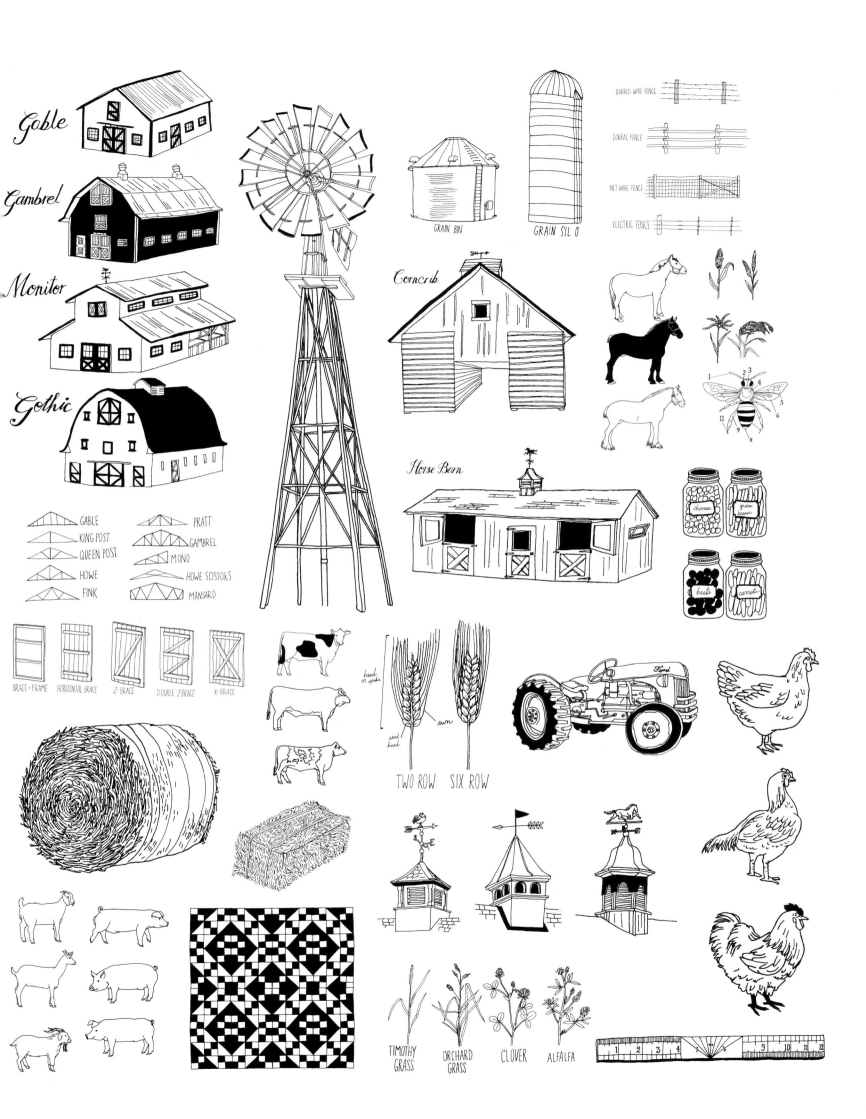

Gable

Gambrel

Monitor

Gothic

GABLE
KING POST
QUEEN POST
HOWE
FINK

PRATT
GAMBREL
MONO
HOWE SCISSORS
MANSARD

BRACE + FRAME   HORIZONTAL BRACE   Z-BRACE   DOUBLE Z-BRACE   X-BRACE

GRAIN BIN

GRAIN SIL O

BARBED WIRE FENCE

CORRAL FENCE

NET WIRE FENCE

ELECTRIC FENCE

Corncrib

Horse Barn

cherries    green beans

beets    carrots

head or spike
awn
seed head

TWO ROW    SIX ROW

Ford

TIMOTHY GRASS    ORCHARD GRASS    CLOVER    ALFALFA

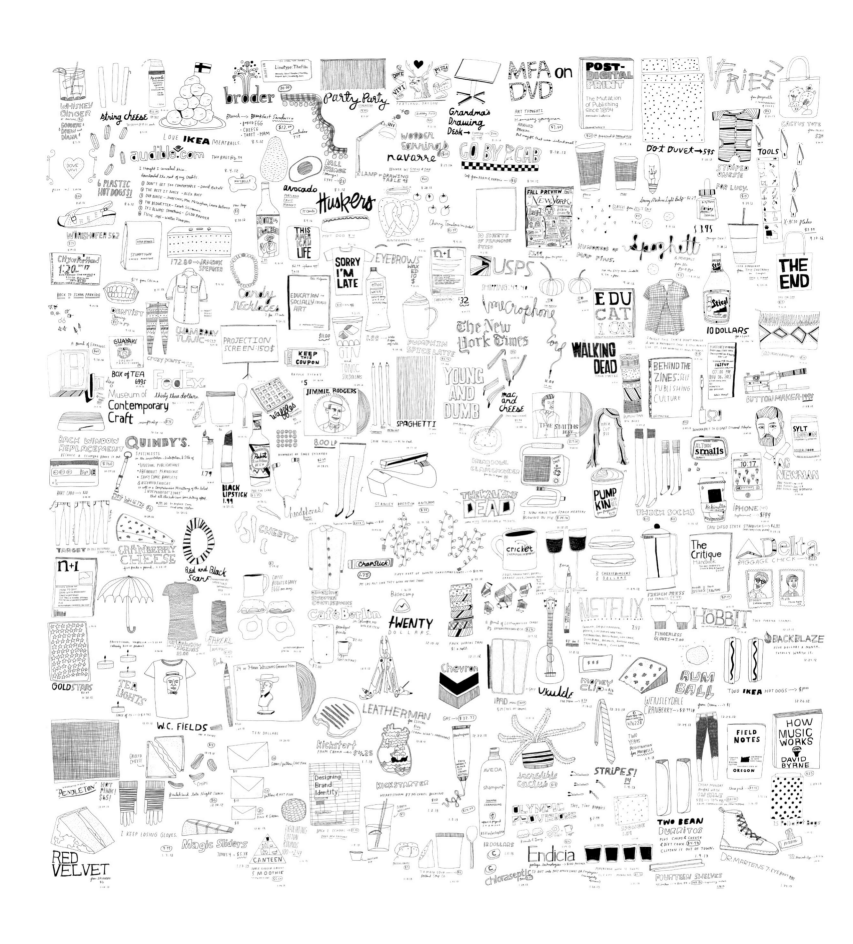

## KATE BINGAMAN-BURT
*DAILY DRAWINGS, 2012*

Kate Bingaman-Burt has here compiled a selection of some of her daily purchases in 2012—she drew one purchased item a day for several years in the context of a project that included a book by the name of **Obsessive Consumption: What Did You Buy Today?** published in 2010. Next to each drawing, Bingaman-Burt has marked what the purchased item is, along with its price and the date on which it was bought.

01

02

03

04

05

06

07

08

09

10

**CHRISTINA CHRISTOFOROU**
*TEN LOVE STORIES, 2013*

This infographic is a visual summary of ten legendary love stories, from Adam & Eve to John Lennon & Yoko Ono. Illustrator Christina Christoforou was interested in finding the symbols that immediately bring these love stories to mind, thereby representing the most dramatic element of each narrative.

JOHN KILBURN
*THE GOLDEN PLAICE, 2012*

John Kilburn was inspired by Victorian nonsense literature and scientific illustrations of Cornish sea life when creating "The Golden Plaice." Another major influence was Samuel Fallours, who published the first color catalogue of fish in 1719. It is estimated that Fallours invented at least 10 percent of the creatures he painted. Together, scientific taxonomy and wild imagination create the ideal counterpoint to produce such works.

MICKEY DUZYJ
*THE FIST PUMP IN TENNIS: A STYLE GUIDE, 2011*

One of the most entertaining parts of watching people play professional tennis is the exaggerated, almost theatrical poses and grunts the players tend to indulge in. This amusing illustration commissioned by ESPN.com is a collection of what Mickey Duzyj calls "fist pumping grandeur."

# GENESIS OF COOKIES

DOCUMENTED HISTORY OF TODAY'S MOST FAMOUS COOKIES FROM DIFFERENT PLACES AND TIME

**BISCOTTI**
ANCIENT ROMAN
1ST CENTURY AD

**YAKGWA**
KOREA
6TH CENTURY AD

**JUMBLE**
MIDDLE EAST
7TH CENTURY AD

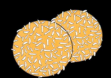

**SESAME SEEDS BALL**
CHINA
7TH CENTURY AD

**PIZZELLE**
ITALY
8TH CENTURY AD

**MACAROON**
ITALY
9TH CENTURY

**GINGERBREAD**
GERMANY
11TH CENTURY

**LADYFINGER**
FRANCE
11TH CENTURY

**ALFAJOR**
PERU
12TH CENTURY

**SHORTBREAD**
UNITED KINGDOM
12TH CENTURY

**SPRINGERLE**
GERMANY
14TH CENTURY

**SPRITZ**
GERMANY
16TH CENTURY

**CHINESE ALMOND COOKIE**
CHINA
16TH CENTURY

**LINZER**
AUSTRIA
17TH CENTURY

**MERINGUE**
UNITED KINGDOM
17TH CENTURY

**SPECULAAS**
NETHERLANDS
17TH CENTURY

**MADELEINE**
FRANCE
18TH CENTURY

**NAZARETH/AMISH SUGAR COOKIE**
UNITED STATES
18TH CENTURY

**CORNSTARCH COOKIE**
BRAZIL
19TH CENTURY

**BROWNIE**
UNITED STATES
19TH CENTURY

**SNICKERDOODLE**
UNITED STATES
19TH CENTURY

**THUMBPRINT**
E. EUROPE OR POLAND OR SWEDEN
19TH CENTURY

**ANIMAL CRACKER**
UNITED KINGDOM
19TH CENTURY

**ANZAC BISCUIT**
AUSTRALIA
20TH CENTURY

**BLACK & WHITE COOKIE**
UNITED STATES
20TH CENTURY

**CHOCOLATE CHIP COOKIE**
UNITED STATES
20TH CENTURY

**FORTUNE COOKIE**
JAPAN
20TH CENTURY

**MACARON**
FRANCE
20TH CENTURY

**PALMIER**
FRANCE
20TH CENTURY

**PEANUT BUTTER COOKIE**
UNITED STATES
20TH CENTURY

**SWEETOOTH**
*GENESIS OF COOKIES, 2014*

"Genesis of Cookies" presents different types of cookies organized chronologically according to the century they were invented in, starting in the first century AD in ancient Rome with the ancestor of the biscotti, and ending in the twentieth century in the United States with the peanut butter cookie.

**POST TYPOGRAPHY**
*POPULAR POSES IN THE SMILEBOOTH, 2012*

Never know what to do inside of a photobooth? Post Typography gives you a few ideas on this poster that was wheatpasted all over Los Angeles promoting a new digital photobooth company. The last space on the bottom right corner was purposefully left blank for people to add their own drawings.

# The Best Pictures

| 1927-28 | 1928-29 | 1929-30 | 1930-31 | 1931-32 | 1932-33 | 1934 | 1935 | 1936 |
|---|---|---|---|---|---|---|---|---|
| 1937 | 1938 | 1939 | 1940 | 1941 | 1942 | 1943 | 1944 | 1945 |
| 1946 | 1947 | 1948 | 1949 | 1950 | 1951 | 1952 | 1953 | 1954 |
| 1955 | 1956 | 1957 | 1958 | 1959 | 1960 | 1961 | 1962 | 1963 |
| 1964 | 1965 | 1966 | 1967 | 1968 | 1969 | 1970 | 1971 | 1972 |
| 1973 | 1974 | 1975 | 1976 | 1977 | 1978 | 1979 | 1980 | 1981 |
| 1982 | 1983 | 1984 | 1985 | 1986 | 1987 | 1988 | 1989 | 1990 |
| 1991 | 1992 | 1993 | 1994 | 1995 | 1996 | 1997 | 1998 | 1999 |
| 2000 | 2001 | 2002 | 2003 | 2004 | 2005 | 2006 | 2007 | 2008 |
| 2009 | 2010 | 2011 | 2012 | 2013 | | | | |

1927-28: Wings; 1928-29: The Broadway Melody; 1929-30: All Quiet on the Western Front; 1930-31: Cimarron; 1931-32: Grand Hotel; 1932-33: Cavalcade; 1934: It Happened One Night; 1935: Mutiny on the Bounty; 1936: The Great Ziegfeld; 1937: The Life of Emile Zola; 1938: You Can't Take It With You; 1939: Gone With the Wind; 1940: Rebecca; 1941: How Green Was My Valley; 1942: Mrs. Miniver; 1943: Casablanca; 1944: Going My Way; 1945: The Lost Weekend; 1946: The Best Years of Our Lives; 1947: Gentlemen's Agreement; 1948: Hamlet; 1949: All the King's Men; 1950: All About Eve; 1951: An American in Paris; 1952: The Greatest Show on Earth; 1953: From Here to Eternity; 1954: On the Waterfront; 1955: Marty; 1956: Around the World in 80 Days; 1957: The Bridge on the River Kwai; 1958: Gigi; 1959: Ben-Hur; 1960: The Apartment; 1961: West Side Story; 1962: Lawrence of Arabia; 1963: Tom Jones; 1964: My Fair Lady; 1965: The Sound of Music; 1966: A Man for All Seasons; 1967: In the Heat of the Night; 1968: Oliver!; 1969: Midnight Cowboy; 1970: Patton; 1971: The French Connection; 1972: The Godfather; 1973: The Sting; 1974: The Godfather Part II; 1975: One Flew Over the Cuckoo's Nest; 1976: Rocky; 1977: Annie Hall; 1978: The Deer Hunter; 1979: Kramer vs. Kramer; 1980: Ordinary People; 1981: Chariots of Fire; 1982: Gandhi; 1983: Terms of Endearment; 1984: Amadeus; 1985: Out of Africa; 1986: Platoon; 1987: The Last Emperor; 1988: Rain Man; 1989: Driving Miss Daisy; 1990: Dances With Wolves; 1991: The Silence of the Lambs; 1992: Unforgiven; 1993: Schindler's List; 1994: Forrest Gump; 1995: Braveheart; 1996: The English Patient; 1997: Titanic; 1998: Shakespeare in Love; 1999: American Beauty; 2000: Gladiator; 2001: A Beautiful Mind; 2002: Chicago; 2003: The Lord of the Rings: The Return of the King; 2004: Million Dollar Baby; 2005: Crash; 2006: The Departed; 2007: No Country for Old Men; 2008: Slumdog Millionaire; 2009: The Hurt Locker; 2010: The King's Speech; 2011: The Artist; 2012: Argo; 2013: 12 Years a Slave

Batman (1989) | Vendetta (2005) | The Mask (1994) | Watchmen (2009) | Gladiator (2000) | Phantom of Paradise (1974)
Lord of the Rings (2003) | Daredevil (2003) | Star Wars (1977) | Clockwork Orange (1971) | Phantom of the Opera (2004)
Nacho Libre (2008) | Predator (2007) | The Mask of Zorro (1989) | 300 (2006) | X-Men (2000) | The Spirit (2009) | Point Break (1991)
Texas Chainsaw Massacre (1974) | Spiderman (2002) | Scream (1996) | Casanova (2005) | The Abominable Dr.Phibes (1971)
Donnie Darko (2001) | Les Yeux sans Visage (1960) | Catwoman (2004) | Amadeus (1984) | Silence of the Lambs (1991)
Friday 13th (1980) | Robocop (1987) | Eyes Wide Shut (1999) | Saw (2004) | Hollow Man (2000) | Star Wars (1977) | 300 (2006)
Iron Man (2008) | Fantômas (1913) | Harry Potter (2007) | Star Wars (1980) | The Mask of Fu Manchu (1932) | Halloween (1978)
The Man with the Iron Mask (1939)

# What's under your Mask?

**BEUTLER INK**
*THE BEST PICTURES, 2014*

Using concise illustrative design and a touch of humor, Beutler Ink has assembled all of the Best Picture winners since the inception of the Academy Awards in 1929. Black and white films are depicted with grayscale icons, while full-color icons represent movies in color.

**ADRIAN PAVIC**
*WHAT'S UNDER YOUR MASK?, 2009*

42 illustrations of iconic masks that have appeared in notable films from 1913 to 2009 can be found on this print by German graphic designer Adrian Pavic. Whether the masks are used to hide someone's identity, to provoke fear in an enemy, or to obscure a terrible disfigurement, they all spark our curiosity, leading us to wonder what lies beneath them.

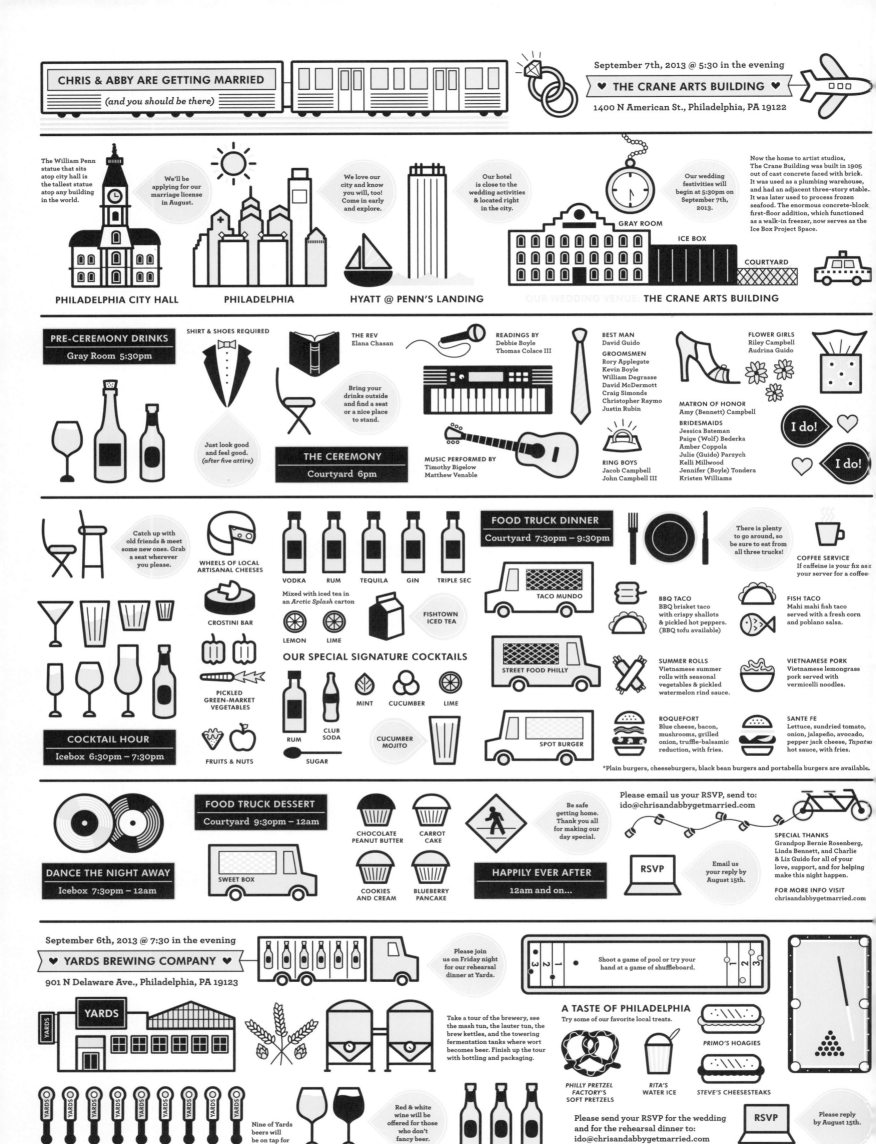

**CHRIS & ABBY ARE GETTING MARRIED**
*(and you should be there)*

September 7th, 2013 @ 5:30 in the evening
♥ **THE CRANE ARTS BUILDING** ♥
1400 N American St., Philadelphia, PA 19122

The William Penn statue that sits atop city hall is the tallest statue atop any building in the world.

We'll be applying for our marriage license in August.

We love our city and know you will, too! Come in early and explore.

Our hotel is close to the wedding activities & located right in the city.

Our wedding festivities will begin at 5:30pm on September 7th, 2013.

Now the home to artist studios, The Crane Building was built in 1905 out of cast concrete faced with brick. It was used as a plumbing warehouse, and had an adjacent three-story stable. It was later used to process frozen seafood. The enormous concrete-block first-floor addition, which functioned as a walk-in freezer, now serves as the Ice Box Project Space.

GRAY ROOM
ICE BOX
COURTYARD

PHILADELPHIA CITY HALL
PHILADELPHIA
HYATT @ PENN'S LANDING
OUR WEDDING VENUE: THE CRANE ARTS BUILDING

**PRE-CEREMONY DRINKS**
Gray Room 5:30pm

SHIRT & SHOES REQUIRED

Just look good and feel good. *(after five attire)*

THE REV
Elana Chasan

Bring your drinks outside and find a seat or a nice place to stand.

**THE CEREMONY**
Courtyard 6pm

READINGS BY
Debbie Boyle
Thomas Colace III

MUSIC PERFORMED BY
Timothy Bigelow
Matthew Venable

BEST MAN
David Guido

GROOMSMEN
Rory Applegate
Kevin Boyle
William Degrasse
David McDermott
Craig Simonds
Christopher Raymo
Justin Rubin

RING BOYS
Jacob Campbell
John Campbell III

FLOWER GIRLS
Riley Campbell
Audrina Guido

MATRON OF HONOR
Amy (Bennett) Campbell

BRIDESMAIDS
Jessica Bateman
Paige (Wolf) Bederka
Amber Coppola
Julie (Guido) Parzych
Kelli Millwood
Jennifer (Boyle) Tondera
Kristen Williams

I do! ♥
♥ I do!

Catch up with old friends & meet some new ones. Grab a seat wherever you please.

WHEELS OF LOCAL ARTISANAL CHEESES
CROSTINI BAR
PICKLED GREEN-MARKET VEGETABLES
FRUITS & NUTS

VODKA  RUM  TEQUILA  GIN  TRIPLE SEC

Mixed with iced tea in an *Arctic Splash* carton

LEMON  LIME

FISHTOWN ICED TEA

**OUR SPECIAL SIGNATURE COCKTAILS**

RUM  CLUB SODA  MINT  CUCUMBER  LIME  SUGAR

CUCUMBER MOJITO

**COCKTAIL HOUR**
Icebox 6:30pm – 7:30pm

**FOOD TRUCK DINNER**
Courtyard 7:30pm – 9:30pm

There is plenty to go around, so be sure to eat from all three trucks!

COFFEE SERVICE
If caffeine is your fix ask your server for a coffee

TACO MUNDO

BBQ TACO
BBQ brisket taco with crispy shallots & pickled hot peppers. (BBQ tofu available)

FISH TACO
Mahi mahi fish taco served with a fresh corn and poblano salsa.

STREET FOOD PHILLY

SUMMER ROLLS
Vietnamese summer rolls with seasonal vegetables & pickled watermelon rind sauce.

VIETNAMESE PORK
Vietnamese lemongrass pork served with vermicelli noodles.

SPOT BURGER

ROQUEFORT
Blue cheese, bacon, mushrooms, grilled onion, truffle-balsamic reduction, with fries.

SANTE FE
Lettuce, sundried tomato, onion, jalapeño, avocado, pepper jack cheese, *Tapatío* hot sauce, with fries.

*Plain burgers, cheeseburgers, black bean burgers and portabella burgers are available.

**FOOD TRUCK DESSERT**
Courtyard 9:30pm – 12am

SWEET BOX

CHOCOLATE PEANUT BUTTER
CARROT CAKE
COOKIES AND CREAM
BLUEBERRY PANCAKE

Be safe getting home. Thank you all for making our day special.

**DANCE THE NIGHT AWAY**
Icebox 7:30pm – 12am

**HAPPILY EVER AFTER**
12am and on...

Please email us your RSVP, send to:
ido@chrisandabbygetmarried.com

RSVP
Email us your reply by August 15th.

SPECIAL THANKS
Grandpop Bernie Rosenberg, Linda Bennett, and Charlie & Liz Guido for all of your love, support, and for helping make this night happen.

FOR MORE INFO VISIT
chrisandabbygetmarried.com

September 6th, 2013 @ 7:30 in the evening
♥ **YARDS BREWING COMPANY** ♥
901 N Delaware Ave., Philadelphia, PA 19123

Please join us on Friday night for our rehearsal dinner at Yards.

Shoot a game of pool or try your hand at a game of shuffleboard.

YARDS

Take a tour of the brewery, see the mash tun, the lauter tun, the brew kettles, and the towering fermentation tanks where wort becomes beer. Finish up the tour with bottling and packaging.

**A TASTE OF PHILADELPHIA**
Try some of our favorite local treats.

PHILLY PRETZEL FACTORY'S SOFT PRETZELS
RITA'S WATER ICE
PRIMO'S HOAGIES
STEVE'S CHEESESTEAKS

Nine of Yards beers will be on tap for you to try.

Red & white wine will be offered for those who don't fancy beer.

Please send your RSVP for the wedding and for the rehearsal dinner to:
ido@chrisandabbygetmarried.com

RSVP
Please reply by August 15th.

**ABBY RYAN DESIGN**
*CHRIS & ABBY GET MARRIED, 2013*

An innovative invitation and program condensed into one, this screen print lists all of the events of Chris and Abby's wedding, from the hotel the guests will be staying at to the entire menu of food available from the four different food trucks during the reception. All 200 guests received this memorable invitation.

**KOMBOH**
*MIYAZAKI'S EYES, 2013*

Intended as a tribute to Hayao Miyazaki's work, this print is a collection of characters from various Studio Ghibli films. KOMBOH has presented the cast in static form, staring past both the viewer and one another.

# D
**Mais**

Cinema

# TURURURURU RURURURURU TURURURURU ...BATMAN!

Estreia amanhã o último filme da trilogia do Batman realizada por Christopher Nolan com Christian Bale na pele do homem-morcego. "O Cavaleiro das Trevas Renasce" chega a Portugal depois de uma estreia atribulada nos EUA, com antestreias especiais hoje à meia--noite em alguns cinemas. Os fãs limpam as lágrimas das saudades que já sentem deste que é, para muitos, o melhor Batman até hoje. Juntámos os oito filmes numa só infografia, adicionámos algumas informações úteis e muitas mais inúteis e o resultado foi este. Um guia enciclopédico para o universo Batman

**DIANA GARRIDO** *diana.garrido@ionline.pt*
**CARLOS MONTEIRO** *carlos.monteiro@ionline.pt*

**2012** — O MAU MAIS MAU (EM BOM) DE TODA A HISTÓRIA DOS MAUS · BANE · A CATWOMAN DE ANNE HATHAWAY, ALÉM DE BOA (E NÃO FALAMOS DE CARÁCTER), TAMBÉM TEM CONSCIÊNCIA · CATWOMAN · JOSEPH GORDON-LEVITT ESTÁ PARA O INSPECTOR GORDON COMO ROBIN ESTÁ PARA O BATMAN, MAS SEM SER RIDÍCULO · BLAKE · GARY OLDMAN SERIA INCRÍVEL ATÉ A FAZER DE WILLY WONKA · **2012**

**2008** — O JOKER DE HEATH LEDGER: MEDO. MUITO MEDO · JOKER · A SÓNIA BRAZÃO TAMBÉM FOI PELOS ARES E NÃO FOI POR ISSO QUE SE TRANSFORMOU NUMA VILÃ · DUAS CARAS · BALE, A FUMAR CIGARROS DESDE O "IMPÉRIO DO SOL" PARA FICAR COM ESTA VOZ · HARVEY DENT · **2008**

**2005** — CILLIAN MURPHY, MUITO BOM A FAZER DE MAU · ESPANTALHO · LIAM NEESON INTERPRETA O ÚNICO VILÃO QUE SE SABE VESTIR · RA'S AL GHUL · CHRISTIAN BALE, ONDE ESTIVESTE ESTE TEMPO TODO? · SE ESTE ALFRED DE MICHAEL CAINE NÃO É O MELHOR DE SEMPRE, DIGAM-NOS LÁ QUAL É · ALFRED · COMISSÁRIO GORDON · MORGAN FREEMAN FAZ DE MORGAN FREEMAN INVENTOR · LUCIUS FOX · **2005**

**1997** — ARNOLD DEVIA TER-SE DEDICADO À POLÍTICA ANTES DESTE DISPARATE · DR. FREEZE · NESTE FILME, É TUDO TÃO MAU QUE ESTAR AQUI A BATER NA UMA THURMAN SERIA UM DESPERDÍCIO DE TEMPO MAIOR DO QUE O QUE LEVOU A ESCREVER ISTO · POISON IVY · BANE? ÉS TU? PARA VER UM BANE A SÉRIO VÁ AMANHÃ AO CINEMA · BANE · ATÉ GEORGE CLOONEY SABE QUE FOI O PIOR BATMAN DE TODOS · RIDÍCULO MAS COM UM FATO DIFERENTE · ROBIN · NÃO HÁ PALAVRAS PARA DESCREVER ALICIA SILVERSTONE... ESPERA: R-I-D-Í-C-U-L-A · BATGIRL · **1997**

**1995** — COM JOEL SCHUMACHER A REALIZAR, NEM TOMMY LEE JONES SE SAFA · DUAS CARAS · COM JOEL SCHUMACHER A REALIZAR, NEM JIM CARREY SE SAFA · ENIGMA · VAL KILMER, O SEGUNDO PIOR BATMAN DE SEMPRE · RIDÍCULO MESMO SEM O "R" · ROBIN · **1995**

**1992** — ATÉ PERCEBEMOS PORQUE É QUE OS PAIS O ABANDONARAM · PINGUIM · MICHELLE PFEIFFER ERA A MELHOR CATWOMAN ATÉ APARECER A OUTRA LÁ DE CIMA. MAS É BOA. BEM BOA · CATWOMAN · **1992**

**1989** — O ÚNICO JOKER QUE SE RIA FACE AO PERIGO · JOKER · É UM PINGUIM QUE SE PODE LEVAR PARA QUALQUER LADO, AO CONTRÁRIO DO PINGUIM DE DANNY DEVITO NÃO SUJA NADA · TINHA CARA DE QUEM NÃO FAZIA MAL A UMA MOSCA MAS ERA MENTIRA · MICHAEL KEATON, O MELHOR BATMAN A SEGUIR A CHRISTIAN BALE (TAMBÉM SÓ HOUVE CINCO) · SE ESTE NÃO É O ALFRED MAIS FOFINHO, NÃO SABEMOS QUEM SERÁ · ALFRED · SE ESTE NÃO É O GORDON MAIS GORDINHO, NÃO SABEMOS QUEM SERÁ · COMISSÁRIO GORDON · **1989**

**1966** — FUGIU DO CIRCO E JUNTOU-SE AOS VILÕES, MAS ESQUECEU-SE DE TIRAR A ROUPA E MAQUILHAGEM · JOKER · PINGUIM · CATWOMAN · UM VILÃO QUE PODIA SER O EDITOR DO CRUZADEX · ENIGMA · O ÚNICO BATMAN SEM ABDOMINAIS · O "R" É DE RIDÍCULO · ROBIN · ALFRED · COMISSÁRIO GORDON · **1966**

# O MELHOR DE KURT COBAIN

O líder dos Nirvana foi encontrado morto em casa a 8 de Abril de 1994. O relatório da polícia haveria de confirmar o suicídio do músico três dias antes. 20 anos depois, Kurt Cobain é ainda um dos mais influentes ícones do rock'n'roll, graças a um inegável legado criativo e a uma imagem que não falha em marcar sucessivas gerações. Juntamos as duas dimensões do artista e recordamos alguns dos momentos essenciais de uma das figuras mais marcantes da cultura popular

TIAGO PEREIRA (Textos) *tiago.pereira@ionline.pt* CARLOS MONTEIRO (Ilustração) *carlos.monteiro@ionline.pt*

Kurt Donald Cobain nasceu a 20 de Fevereiro de 1967 em Aberdeen, no estado de Washington. A música apareceu pouco depois

O Sears Bass com que gravou algumas das primeiras demos haveria de fazer sucesso em leilão, vendido por mais de 40 mil dólares

A 23 de Julho de 1985, Kurt Cobain foi preso por vandalismo. Escreveu numa parede, com spray: "Ain'T goT no how waTchamacalliT"

No palco do Astoria, Londres, 1989, quando os Nirvana integraram a digressão europeia da editora Sub Pop

No bar Raji's, Hollywood, 1990. Ou a melhor forma de acabar um concerto, não há como voltar atrás

A malha às riscas ficou famosa e fez moda. É a mesma que aparece no teledisco de "Sliver", single de 1990

Texas, 1991: Kurt faz um stage dive; o segurança puxa-o; Cobain não gosta e dá-lhe com a guitarra; o segurança esmurra-o; caos

"Smells Like Teen Spirit", o primeiro single de "Nevermind", álbum de 1991 que transformou os Nirvana num fenómeno e Kurt num ídolo

De pernas para o ar, em Março de 1991. Apesar do aparato, acabou tudo bem. Charles Peterson fez do momento uma foto clássica

A jogar em casa, num concerto gravado no Paramount Theater de Seattle, o único dos Nirvana rodado em filme de 16 milímetros

No teledisco de "Come as You Are", a canção que levou muitos a aprender a tocar guitarra – a maioria não passou da quarta nota

"Lithium". Foi o terceiro single de "Nevermind". Era mais difícil de tocar, tinha muitos acordes, não estávamos preparados

"In Bloom", com o nosso herói dividido entre o músico penteado e bem comportado e o punk sem remédio

Com o vestido de baile para o Headbangers Ball, da MTV. "Toda a gente quer estar na moda", disse sobre a febre Nirvana de 1991

Os Nirvana em números – Dave Grohl: 1,83 metros; Kurt Cobain: 1,77 metros; Krist Novoselic: 2,01 metros

A T-shirt que usou nos Video Music Awards de 1992, com a capa do álbum-cassete de Daniel Johnston, "Hi, How Are You"

Ao vivo no festival de Reading, Inglaterra, em 1992. Há um CD e um DVD para nos lembrar que devíamos ter lá estado

No final do concerto no Hollywood Rock Festival, no Rio de Janeiro, vestido de mulher, como fez muitas outras vezes

"Heart Shaped Box", o primeiro single de "In Utero", álbum de 1993. O vídeo foi realizado pelo holandês Anton Corbijn

Kurt conheceu Courtney em 1990; casaram em Fevereiro de 1992; Frances Bean Cobain nasceu em Agosto do mesmo ano

Para a entrevista a Kurt Loder, o mesmo que interrompeu a programação da MTV meses mais tarde para anunciar a morte de Cobain

No MTV Live and Loud de 1993. Os Pearl Jam também faziam parte do cartaz mas Eddie Vedder estava com gripe

Noite das Bruxas, 1993, Akron, Ohio: Kurt Cobain actua vestido de Barney, o Dinossauro, personagem infantil da TV americana

Sentado, no unplugged gravado em Nova Iorque: quem ainda não tinha dado pelos Nirvana não escapou a isto

Os Nirvana actuaram em Portugal a 6 de Fevereiro de 1994, no Dramático de Cascais. Kurt Cobain morreu ois meses depois

## I INFOGRAFIA

The print to the left depicts the evolution of the Batman movie franchise, showing how the main characters have been changing since 1966. On the right, a humorous chronological illustration of Kurt Cobain's life and career is shown, with commentary in Portuguese. Clothes, attitudes, and musical instruments help tell the story of one of the most influential musicians of the 1990s.

**ROBERT M BALL**
*40 BADDIES/40 GOODIES, 2013*

Lord Voldemort and the Wicked Witch of the West on one side, Spider-Man and Edward Scissorhands on the other: "40 Baddies/40 Goodies" is a graphic representation of the age-old Good vs. Evil dichotomy.

THE SPAGHETTI WESTERN INVENTORY

# PITT
## "The Square"

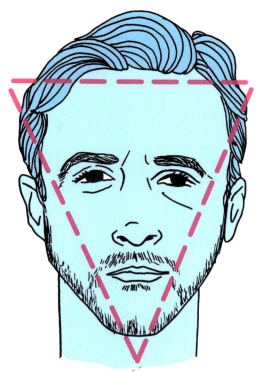

# GOSLING
## "The Triangle"

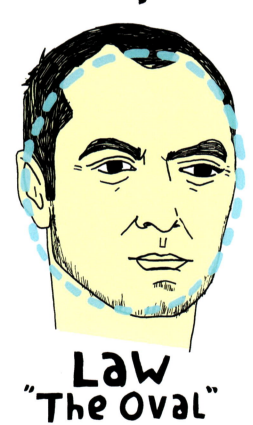

# Law
## "The Oval"

# Pattinson
## "The Diamond"

**MAX DALTON**
*THE SPAGHETTI WESTERN INVENTORY, 2010*

Assembling archetypal characters and objects from spaghetti western films–a term used to designate a genre of westerns primarily produced and directed by Italians during the 1960s and 70s–Max Dalton has designed an inventory that includes everything from the get-off-my-property shotgun to the wooden, swinging saloon doors.

**RICHARD FAIRHEAD**
*SHAPE FACE, 2013*

Do you have a circular face with full cheeks and a rounded chin? Or a heart-shaped face with a broad forehead tapering to a small, neat chin and mouth? A rectangular shape, with a square chin, quite a strong jaw line, and possibly a longer nose? Or perhaps you are more like the Law type with an oval face, and a rounded chin and forehead? Illustrator Richard Fairhead drew this guide for online men's style magazine **The Chic Geek** to help men find the perfect type of eyewear. Try it!

# Ten great years

MAX DALTON
*TEN GREAT YEARS & GUITAR LESSONS,
2011 / 2009*

"Ten Great Years" is a visual timeline of the Beatles based on their drastic style changes throughout the years, including a subtle appearance by Yoko Ono. To the right, "Guitar Lessons" illustrates the best rock guitar players of all time, starting with Frank Zappa and ending with Peter Green.

# Guitar lessons

## A series of master classes

given by:

Frank Zappa, George Harrison, Slash, Jimi Hendrix, Keith Richards, Jimmy Page, Stevie Ray Vaughan, Eric Clapton, Mark Knopfler, Brian May, Johnny Ramone, Jack White, The Edge, Chuck Berry, Angus Young, Pete Townshend, Tony Iommi, Eddie Van Halen, David Gilmour, Ace Frehley, Ritchie Blackmore, Duane Allman, Kirk Hammett, Carlos Santana, John Frusciante, Yngwie Malmsteen, Kurt Cobain, Mike Bloomfield, Jerry Garcia, Ry Cooder, Bo Diddley, Jeff Beck, Tom Morello, Brian Setzer and Peter Green.

# WES ANDERSON'S HAPPY FAMILIES PLAYING CARDS

## MAX DALTON

*WES ANDERSON'S HAPPY FAMILIES PLAYING CARDS & PULP FICTION ACTION FIGURE COLLECTION, 2012/2010*

Whether it be precocious Margot Tenenbaum, heart-broken Jack Whitman, or eccentric Steve Zissou, everyone who has seen Wes Anderson's films has surely fallen in love with one of the beautifully idiosyncratic characters he brings to life. Buenos Aires-based graphic artist Max Dalton imagined a card game inspired by Anderson's oeuvre, from **Bottle Rocket** to **Moonrise Kingdom.** In the same naïve aesthetic that is his trademark, Dalton created a print featuring the characters from Quentin Tarantino's **Pulp Fiction** as action figures.

# PULP FICTION
## Action Figure Collection

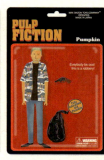

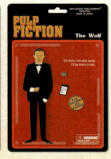

Max Dalton

# FISH EATERS OF THE WORLD

### NEW ENGLAND CRAB CRUNCHER

A curious species native to the Northeastern United States, they're easily caught with North Atlantic Oysters, Dungeness Crab or Live Lobster.

### CORPORATE SHARK

The Corporate Shark can be found primarily in trendy environments. She feeds mainly on Sushi, Swordfish and Oysters on the Half Shell.

### LARGEMOUTH YUPPIE

The Largemouth Yuppie congregates in urban areas. Reel him in with Copper River Salmon, Mahi Mahi and Alaskan King Crab.

### BACKCOUNTRY TRAILWALKER

The Backcountry Trailwalker avoids populated areas, but congregates in "green" grocery stores and restaurants. Reel him in with MSC certified sustainable products, including Oregon Pink Shrimp, Pacific Halibut and New Zealand Hoki.

### MUSCLES

Muscles can be found in nearly any restaurant environment, usually in close proximity to a gym. Catch and release with Pacific Halibut, Shrimp, Scallops or any other high-protein, low-fat fish.

### DESERT DWELLER

The Desert Dweller can be found in traditional Southwestern restaurants. They avoid exotic fish, but are easily caught with grilled Rainbow Trout, Atlantic Salmon and Catfish.

### THE SPONGE

Found in schools, the Sponge soaks up knowledge while feeding on brain food. You'll catch them with sustainable omega-3 fish like grilled Salmon, Herring and Mackerel.

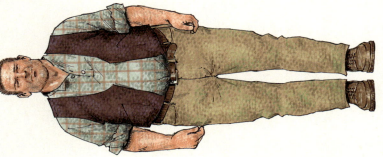

### PUB CRAWLER

The Pub Crawler feeds primarily on fried foods. Ideal baits include Catfish, Popcorn Shrimp and Calamari.

### TEENAGE GROUPER

The Teenage Grouper travels in groups of similar individuals. They're easy to hook with Gulf Shrimp, Tilapia or any other quick-serve fish.

### PACIFIC COAST TRANSPLANT

The Pacific Coast Transplant migrated from large, West Coast cities and is attracted to any trendy, upscale restaurant. Lure her in with Albacore Tuna, Pacific Rockfish and Santa Barbara Prawns.

### SUNBAKED SAMARITAN

You'll find the Sunbaked Samaritan in environmentally balanced restaurants and stores. Catch him with sustainable MSC seafood like Gulf of Alaska Pacific Cod, US North Pacific Sablefish and Patagonian Scallops.

### ENLIGHTENED EPICUREAN

The Enlightened Epicurean can be found in environmentally conscious grocery stores and restaurants. She feeds exclusively on MSC sustainable fish, such as Alaskan Salmon, South Georgia Patagonian Toothfish and Pacific American Albacore Tuna.

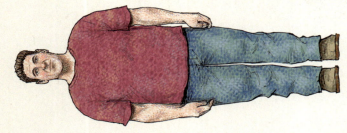

### GULF COAST SWAMP DWELLER

Native to the Gulf of Mexico, this species has a unique palette. They feed primarily on Cajun Crawfish, Catfish and Wahoo.

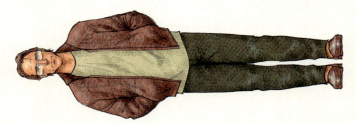

### FEARLESS GOBBLER

The Fearless Gobbler isn't a picky eater. He'll often eat prey more timid creatures would pass up. Reel him in with Whole Crawfish, Alligator, Monkfish and Conch.

Seattle Fish Company provides the Southwest's largest variety of high-quality fresh and frozen fish. So no matter what pond you're fishing in, we've got the bait for you.

Catch more customers.

Seattle Fish Company of New Mexico, Inc. 2500 Comanche Rd. NE, Albuquerque, NM 87107 | 505.888.6969 | seattlefishnm.com

# ENSEMBLE

## THE STYLE OF MUSIC

(Left - Right)  Jim Morrison   Johnny Cash   Kurt Cobain   Kiss   Chet Baker   Michael Jackson   Run DMC   Jimi Hendrix   Bob Dylan   Elvis Presley   Prince   Kanye West   Marvin Gaye   The Ramones
Andre 3000   Pharrell Williams   Brandon Flowers   Pete Doherty   The Beatles   Miles Davis

Moxy

AD: Moxy Creative

## 3 ADVERTISING

*SEATTLE FISH COMPANY OF NEW MEXICO POSTER, 2012*

In a humorous twist on the common "fish poster," 3 Advertising has replaced the different types of fish with different types of fish-eaters. The poster was designed to be distributed to chefs and restaurant owners, reminding them that SFCNM are not just fish experts, they are also skilled when it comes to helping their clients catch more customers.

## ALEX MATHERS

*ENSEMBLE: THE STYLE OF MUSIC, 2010*

"Ensemble: The Style of Music" is a series of illustrations created by Toronto-based PRODUCT magazine's lead designer that depicts 20 famous musicians by focusing on a single iconic outfit that each has worn.

FENDER
ELECTRIC INSTRUMENT CO.

Jacob Borshard

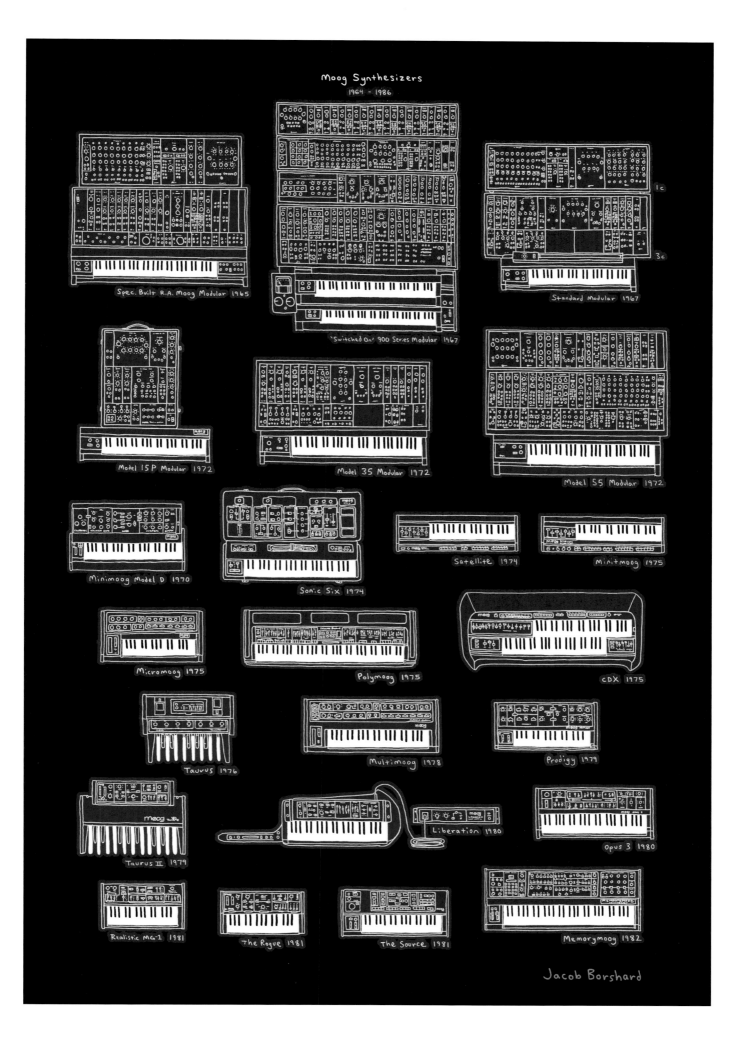

**Moog Synthesizers**
1964 - 1986

Spec. Built R.A. Moog Modular 1965

"Switched On" 900 Series Modular 1967

Standard Modular 1967

Model 15P Modular 1972

Model 35 Modular 1972

Model 55 Modular 1972

Minimoog Model D 1970

Sonic Six 1974

Satellite 1974

Minitmoog 1975

Micromoog 1975

Polymoog 1975

CDX 1975

Taurus 1976

Multimoog 1978

Prodigy 1979

Taurus II 1979

Liberation 1980

Opus 3 1980

Realistic MG-1 1981

The Rogue 1981

The Source 1981

Memorymoog 1982

Jacob Borshard

## JACOB BORSHARD

*FENDER ELECTRIC INSTRUMENT CO. & MOOG SYNTHESIZERS 2014*

Jacob Borshard's love of music here translates into two detailed screen prints: "Fender Electric Instrument Co." compiles every classic Fender guitar model and amplifier in chronological order (including a few prototypes), and "Moog Synthesizers" charts every production synthesizer (and a sampling of the evolution of custom modular types) created by the original Moog Music, also in chronological order.

### GRID

*A STUDIO LIFE, 2012*

Graphic designer and art director Ashwin Patel designed this elegant poster with 42 illustrations representing the typical life of a design studio in a figurative sense. Some of the images have an emotional connotation covering everything from "pressure" to "recognition," while others depict studio activities in a tongue-in-cheek way, such as "pitching," which Patel paired with the image of a flask.

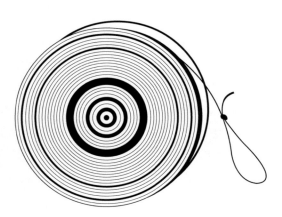

# A studio life.

| PRESSURE | SPINNING | STICKY FINGERS | MISCHIEF | DISTURBING REPS | RELEASE |
|---|---|---|---|---|---|

| ENVY | CUTBACKS | LITTLE TREASURES | HEART | PURISTS | MATHEMATICS |
|---|---|---|---|---|---|

| GOOD COMPANY | REFERENCES | TALENTS | THE UPS AND DOWNS | DECEPTION | EVOLVE |
|---|---|---|---|---|---|

| PRECAUTIONS | HEROS | EGOS | DISCOVERY | SACRIFICE | CONTACTS |
|---|---|---|---|---|---|

| RESPONSIBILITY | MENTORS | HALLUCINOGENICS | CHARACTERS | IMAGES | SURVIVAL |
|---|---|---|---|---|---|

| SIGNIFICANCE | RECOGNITION | OLD TIMERS | HERBAL REMEDIES | FREELANCERS | PITCHING |
|---|---|---|---|---|---|

| GREAT LUNCHES | MARKETING DEPARTMENT | PRESENTATION | INFLUENCE | BUILD | CLIENTS |
|---|---|---|---|---|---|

MARCO GORAN ROMANO
NOT FOR RENTAL, 2013

The United States Postal Service does not have an official motto, but there is an inscription on the James Farley Post Office in New York City that reads "Neither snow nor rain nor heat nor gloom of night stays these couriers from the swift completion of their appointed rounds." This quote, translated from ancient Greek, appears on this print as a tribute to Kevin Costner's 1997 film The Postman.

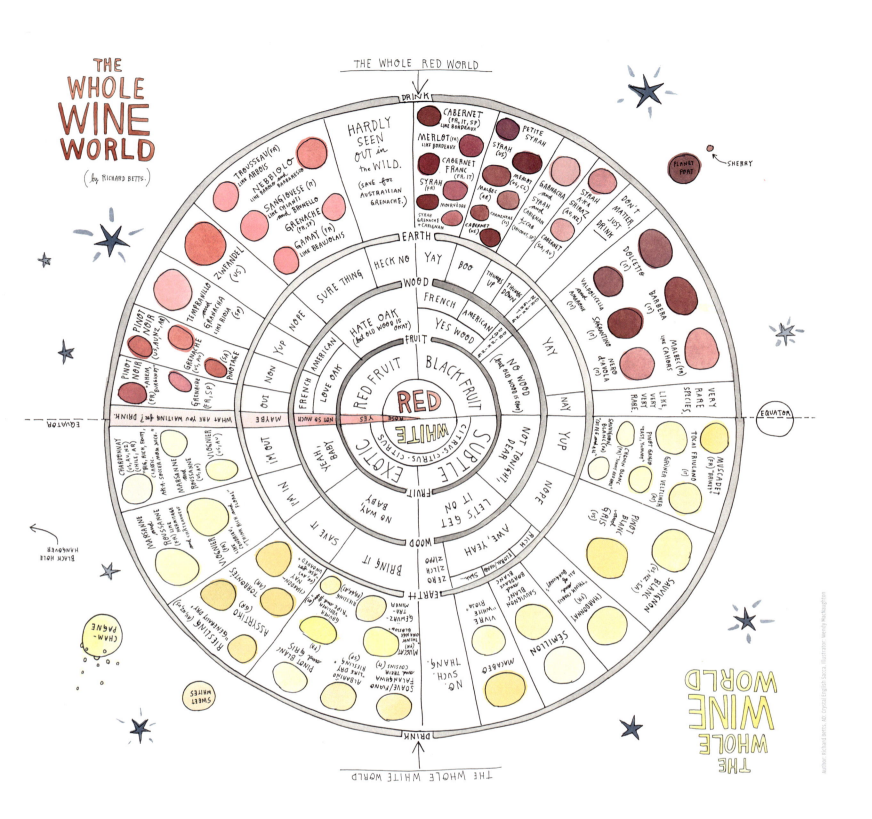

WENDY MACNAUGHTON
*THE WHOLE WINE WORLD, 2013*

"The Whole Wine World" breaks down the world's red and white wines into a few simple categories–fruit, wood, and earth–to help people better understand wine and discover what they like and why. Each color on the wheel matches the shade of the corresponding wine, and was painted using wine and watercolors. The print was created as a collaborative effort between master sommelier Richard Betts, art director Crystal English Sacca, and illustrator Wendy MacNaughton, and was published in their book **The Essential Scratch and Sniff Guide to Becoming A Wine Expert.**

# Canadian Constellations

OH **CANADIAN SKYS AT NIGHT:** May these heavenly bodies guide you home or safely into a ditch should a moose decide to dance mid-highway.

| | | | | |
|---|---|---|---|---|
| 01 Black Gold of Horton | 06 The Looner Landing | 11 Bob's CGI Supercluster | 16 The Good Ol' Dipper | 21 Intergalactic Arm Wrestler |
| 02 Northern Narwhal Nebula | 07 Black Gold of Hellberta | 12 The Buttermilky Way | 17 Bureaucratic Wonderland | 22 The Dressup Dipper |
| 03 Back Bacon Borealis | 08 The Great One Galaxy | 13 Failed Attempt Avronova | 18 Conrad Black Hole | 23 #ifiHadGlassUpNorthEh |
| 04 Party in the Far Far Back | 09 Crime Fighting Photo Ops | 14 Hold The Hormones | 19 Ordinary Newfoundlander | 24 Liquid Gold Nº 2 |
| 05 Hogged Stone System | 10 The Other Stick Thing | 15 Ogopo-where-did-you-go? | 20 Slap Shooting Stars | 25 The Original Space Jam |

SUPER IMPORTANT INFORMATION • POSTER SIZE: 0.027870012 KM² • POSTER WEIGHT: 0.026349523 KG • DISTANCE TO SUN: WAY FAR • STARDATE OF CREATION: -309326.7154680365 • CONSTELLATIONS OMITTED FROM THIS PRINTING: NORTH OF 60, THE GHOST OF RITA MACNEIL AND THE MYRIAD OF OTHER GOLD NUGGETS OF CANADIAN PLOP CULTURE • LOVINGLY & PAINSTAKINGLY CRAFTED BY KOMBOH

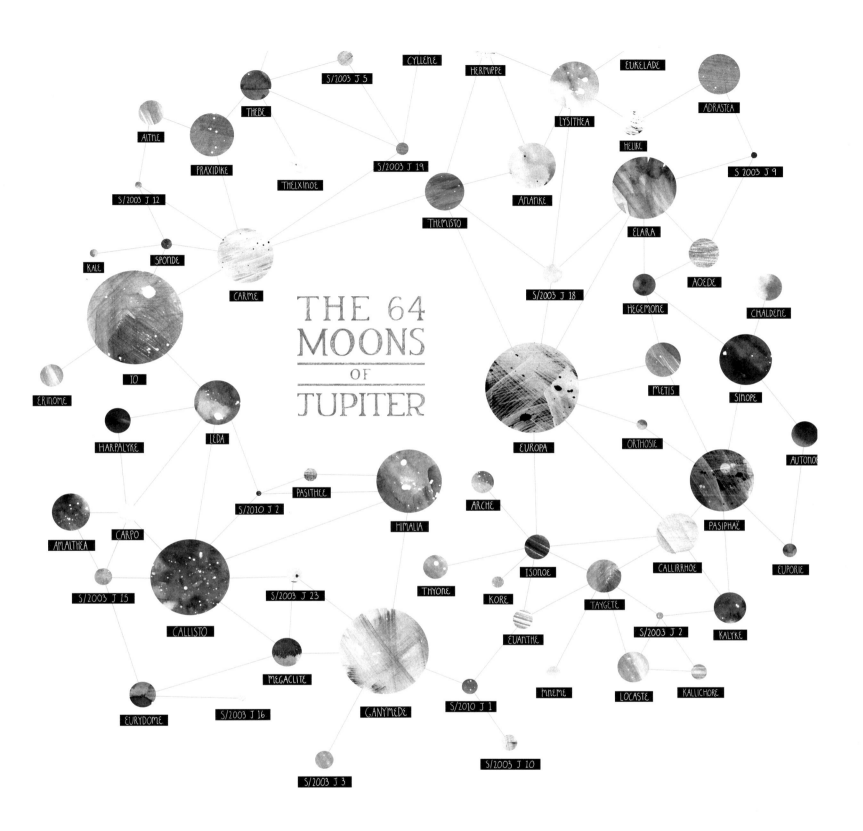

THE 64
MOONS
OF
JUPITER

CYLLENE
S/2003 J 5
HERMIPPE
EUKELADE
ADRASTEA
THEBE
AITHE
LYSITHEA
PRAXIDIKE
HELIKE
S/2003 J 9
THELXINOE
S/2003 J 19
ANANKE
ELARA
S/2003 J 12
THEMISTO
KALE
SPONDE
AOEDE
HEGEMONE
CHALDENE
CARME
IO
EUROPA
METIS
SINOPE
ERINOME
ORTHOSIE
AUTONOE
LEDA
HARPALYKE
S/2003 J 18
PASITHEE
ARCHE
PASIPHAË
S/2010 J 2
HIMALIA
CALLIRRHOE
EUPORIE
CARPO
AMALTHEA
ISONOE
THYONE
TAYGETE
S/2003 J 15
KORE
S/2003 J 2
KALYKE
S/2003 J 23
EVANTHE
CALLISTO
MEGACLITE
MNEME
LOCASTE
KALLICHORE
EURYDOME
S/2003 J 16
GANYMEDE
S/2010 J 1
S/2003 J 10
S/2003 J 3

NICKNAMES: STACHE, MO, MUSTACHIO, SOUP STRAINER, LIP SWEATER, COOKIE DUSTER

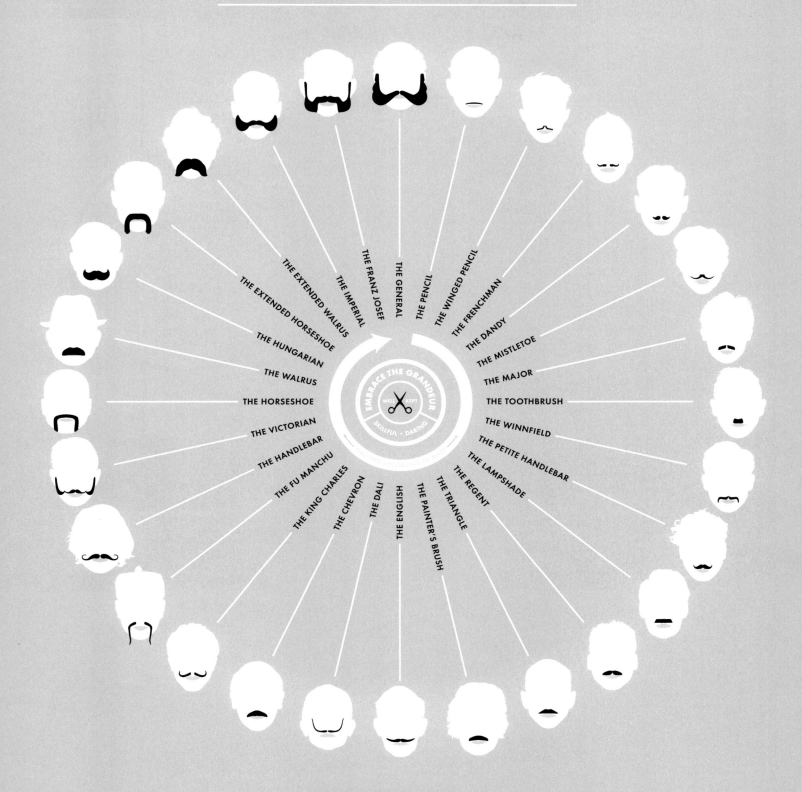

## THE SPECTRUM OF
# MOUSTACHES

**CHARLEY CHARTWELL**
*WILL I MAKE A GOOD SUPERHERO? &
THE SPECTRUM OF MOUSTACHES,
2014/2013*

Inspired by the elaborate display of information in ledgers, instructional charts, and tax forms, the humorous visual aid on this page helps aspiring superheroes foresee the big changes that await them. Through illustrations, charts, and questions, the poster summarizes the day-to-day benefits and drawbacks of becoming a superhero. On the right, another visual aid by the creatives behind Charley Chartwell has made it easy for us to learn the names of all the different moustaches, encouraging men to "embrace the grandeur" of the 'stache. Everybody knows "The Dalí" and "The Toothbrush," but did you recognize "The Mistletoe" or "The Imperial"?

# VISUAL FAMILIES

GRAPHIC STORYTELLING IN DESIGN AND ILLUSTRATION

This book was conceived, edited, and designed by Gestalten.

Edited by Antonis Antoniou, Hendrik Hellige, Sven Ehmann, and Robert Klanten
Introduction by Noelia Hobeika
Texts by Noelia Hobeika and Vanessa Obrecht

Cover graphics by Max Dalton
Layout by Michelle Kliem and Hendrik Hellige
Typefaces: Calcine by Mark Froemberg, foundry: www.gestaltenfonts.com;
Avant Garde Gothic by Herb Lubalin & Tom Carnase

Proofreading by Michael Eisenbrey
Printed by Eberl Print, Immenstadt
Made in Germany

Published by Gestalten, Berlin 2014
ISBN 978-3-89955-540-0

For more information, please visit www.gestalten.com.

Bibliographic information published by the Deutsche Nationalbibliothek. The Deutsche National-bibliothek lists this publication in the Deutsche Nationalbibliografie; detailed bibliographic data are available online at http://dnb.d-nb.de.

None of the content in this book was published in exchange for payment by commercial parties or designers; Gestalten selected all included work based solely on its artistic merit.

This book was printed on paper certified according to the standard of FSC®.

Gestalten is a climate-neutral company. We collaborate with the non-profit carbon offset provider myclimate (www.myclimate.org) to neutralize the company's carbon footprint produced through our worldwide business activities by investing in projects that reduce $CO_2$ emissions (www.gestalten.com/myclimate).